CU01011157

Sevenoaks
A Remarkable Town

By

Elizabeth Purves
Geraldine Tucker
Keith Wade

DESIGN: Victoria Granville Baxter
FRONT COVER PAINTING: Roger FitzGerald
PHOTOGRAPHERS: Martin and Veronica Coath

FOR THE SEVENOAKS SOCIETY

Silver Pines Press
2 Pinewood Ave, Sevenoaks TN14 5AF

ACKNOWLEDGEMENTS

SEVENOAKS TOWN COUNCIL SPONSORSHIP

We are exceedingly grateful to the Sevenoaks Town Council who have given us a generous grant towards the costs of publishing this book.

The following have very kindly taken or given material, photographs and other images for us to use:

Victoria Granville Baxter, CgMs Consulting, Barry Dennis, Roger FitzGerald, Russell Harper, Knocker and Foskett, Jackson-Stops Sevenoaks, Roger Lee, Tim Pearce, Jim Purves, Sevenoaks Library, Sevenoaks Town Council, Alan Surry, The Sevenoaks Society, Ed Thompson, The National Trust - Nathalie Cohen & John Miller, Angus Tucker, Graham Usher, Keith Wade and Michael Willsher.

Thanks are due to Keith Smith for Photoshop and to Alexander Tucker, Angus Tucker and Richard Baxter for Proof reading.

We are also grateful to those owners of featured properties who have provided information, granted access and given permission for photographs to be taken.

Foreword by
SIR MICHAEL HARRISON
President of the Sevenoaks Society

This book is about Sevenoaks and its people. From the earliest reference to Sevenoaks in Bishop Ernulf's 'Textus Roffensis' compiled c.1120, the 900-year history of the Town is traced to the present day by means of its heritage buildings, artefacts and open spaces such as the Vine cricket ground. A stunning array of photographs, both modern and old, accompany the text.

King Henry VIII's manor of Knole, John Donne's Church of St Nicholas and William Sevenoke's Free Grammar School form the first part of this book together with the historic Town centre. The story continues with the great landed estates which surrounded and dominated the Town. These are depicted together with their farms for this was an agricultural-based economy until the 19th century, although the coaching inns and the public houses of this time also have their own tale to tell. Sevenoaks remained a small rural market town until the railway arrived in the 1860s. Its impact was life-changing. A group of remarkable individuals arrived who helped transform Sevenoaks and shaped it into the Town it is today.

The conservation message in the final part of the book is that we ignore the diversity of our heritage at our peril. We need to protect and enhance the features and the characteristics that make Sevenoaks distinctive. But we also need to encourage and recognise buildings and projects which demonstrate excellence in design and construction quality and make a positive impact on the Town.

CONTENTS

TIME LINE

c.1120 Earliest reference to the parish of Sevenoaks in Bishop Ernulf's 'Textus Roffensis'.

1257   Grant of chantry chapel issued to Henry of Ghent.

1432   William Sevenoke endows Free Grammar School and Almshouses.

1456   Archbishop of Canterbury, Thomas Bourchier, purchases Manor of Knole.

1538   Henry VIII appropriates Knole from Thomas Cranmer.

1604   Thomas Sackville acquires Knole.

1616   John Donne, the poet, appointed Rector of Sevenoaks.

1692   Lady Boswell leaves endowment for education of 12 poor scholars in the town.

1734   First recorded cricket match on The Vine cricket ground

1788   Jane Austen stays with her great uncle at The Red House.

1818   Lady Boswell's school opens in London Road.

1837   Queen Victoria's accession.

1842   The 'Old Market House' built.

1853   Wesleyan Chapel opens in Bank Street.

1858   St John's Baptist Church opens.

1862   2nd June Sevenoaks rail line opens at Bat and Ball.

       30th June Parliamentary sanction to build second rail line to Sevenoaks.

1864   New police station and magistrates court built near The Vine.

1865   St John's United Reformed Church built.

1867   Queen Victoria visits Knole by special train to Bat and Ball.

1868   Second rival Sevenoaks rail line opens at Tubs Hill, London Road.

1871   Sevenoaks Local Board created. Town's first elected body.

1875   School Board for Sevenoaks formed.

1877   Cobden Road Board School opens.

1878/9 Lime Tree Walk built.

1880   St Mary's Church, Kippington opens.

1882   Walthamstow Hall School opens.

1887   Vine Baptist Church opens.

       Great barn of Knole destroyed by fire.

1889   Constitutional Club built.

1894	Sevenoaks Urban District Council (SUDC) formed.
1896	St. Thomas RC Church opens in Granville Road - replaces earlier "Iron Church".
1897	William Thompson gives plot of land for The Drill Hall.
1900	The Beacon School moves to Cross Keys and renamed "The New Beacon."
1901	Emily Jackson House (The Children's Hip Hospital) built.
1902	Seven oak trees planted on Vine cricket ground for Edward VII coronation.
1903	The Sevenoaks Tenants Association set up.
1904	Methodist Church opens in The Drive.
	St Luke's Church opens in Eardley Road.
	The Retreat Almshouses built.
1905	The Carnegie Free Public Library opens.
1906	Greatness Park Cemetery opens.
	Cornwall Hall opens.
1913	SUDC buys Greatness land for first Council housing.
1914	Sevenoaks Swimming Baths opened in Eardley Road.
1919	Sevenoaks Prep school founded.
1920	The Sevenoaks War Memorial erected on the Vine.
1924	Percy Harvey buys Wildernesse land for development.
1927	Bradbourne estate sold for development.
1945	The Granville School founded.
1946	Seven oak trees planted near the Vine Tavern to mark end of World War II.
	Knole House given to National Trust.
1974	Sevenoaks District & Town Councils replace Urban and Rural District Councils.
1986	New Library building opens in Buckhurst Lane.
1987	The Great Storm fells the Oak Trees on the Vine grounds.
1995	Construction of The Undercroft at St Nicholas completed.
2010	Knole Academy formed from Bradbourne Girls & Wildernesse Boys schools.
2013	Trinity School opens.
2017	Weald of Kent Girls Grammar school annex opens.

Manor, Church and School

Geraldine Tucker

The earliest reference to the Parish of Sevenoaks is found in Bishop Ernulf's 'Textus Roffensis', written 900 years ago around 1120. The Parish name was written as 'Seouenaca', a reference to the Town's famous seven oaks.

Following the steep climb up Riverhill to the south of the Town, the scene is dominated initially by the centuries old deer park of Knole on the right. Sevenoaks School buildings then appear on both sides of the Tonbridge Road, leading into the High Street. The imposing Park Grange boarding house is found on the left and other School buildings are on the right, including the 'Old School House' and the Almshouses. Sevenoaks School is one of the oldest lay foundations in England. The School, and adjoining Almshouses, were endowed by William Sevenoke's Will of 1432. A short distance further on, located on the left, close to the edge of the road, is the

Town's ancient Parish Church of St Nicholas, and the nearby former Chantry building. With its prominent tower and surrounding old churchyard, St Nicholas Church visually dominates this part of the High Street. Opposite the Church is the main entrance to the historic building of Knole itself.

Knole's Gate Towers built by King Henry VIII

Bourchier's Tower

Knole House is one of the largest stately homes in England. There is, however, little that can be discerned today of the original, small, early 14th century manor house owned by Roger of Knolle. The process of transforming Knole from minor manor dwelling to one of the finest mansions in Kent, was begun by Thomas Bourchier, Archbishop of Canterbury, when he bought Knole in 1456. Bourchier lavished money on Knole and spent much time there. He rebuilt the house and enclosed a park around it. At the west side of the house, now accessible through the main entrance by the later built Green Court, Bourchier built a massive stone vaulted Gatehouse, known today as Bourchier's Tower, opening onto the Stone Court. At the far side of the Stone Court stood the Great Hall and, beyond it, Bourchier's State Apartments. This was once the heart of an Archbishop's Palace.

Successive Archbishops of Canterbury kept the property until 1538 when King Henry VIII forced Archbishop Thomas Cranmer to hand Knole and its estate to him making Knole a royal palace. This royal connection continued until Thomas Sackville, Earl of Dorset, bought Knole in 1604.

KNOLE

Sir Thomas Sackville was one of the wealthiest landowners in England. Determined to make Knole into a magnificent palace that would both stand as his legacy and display his wealth and power to all, he embarked on a massive building programme and remodelled it largely into the vast mansion it is today. While he succeeded in his aim, he did not live to enjoy it, dying in 1608 shortly after work was complete. Thirteen generations of the Sackville family have lived at Knole since then. However, in the early 20th century, with the era of the country house largely over, a combination of death duties and large bills for repair and maintenance meant that Knole could no longer be kept by one family. Knole was given to the National Trust in 1946 with an endowment towards its maintenance. The Sackville family however retained virtually all of the 1,000 acre park and much of the contents of the house. They were also given a 200 year lease on various private apartments within Knole House itself.

Knole: from the South East

Knole is steeped in romantic myths. One of the most prevalent is that Knole House is a 'Calendar House'. While it is true that Knole possesses seven courts and possibly 52 staircases – the total number of rooms have never been counted - the prosaic fact is that Knole was not built as a 'Calendar House. It has developed organically over the centuries.

KNOLE PARK AND GARDENS

Today the Knole estate covers almost 1,000 acres. At 26 acres alone, Knole may possess the largest walled garden in the country. One of the reasons for its size is likely to be the springs which it encloses. Knole's park is also the last medieval deer park in Kent.

A chain fence largely marks the boundary, although part of the northern section is a 19th century ragstone wall built by Welsh stonemasons. The park, which has never been landscaped, is also a Special Site of Scientific Interest. It contains many natural features, including several trees of great age. Other famous points of interest include the Bird House, an 18th century folly built by the 2nd Duke of Dorset.

Public access dispute and the 1887 fire

For centuries, the people of Sevenoaks by common use have seen the park as an amenity. An attempt in 1883 by Lord Mortimer Sackville to deny local people this right led to general rioting, reported in several national newspapers. Lord Mortimer was forced to back down. Since then, the park has remained open to all. More happily, many local people helped put out the fire in 1887 which destroyed the roof and upper part of the great medieval barn of Knole, adjoining the house itself. Part of the National Trust's 'Inspired by Knole' Project was to restore the roof based on archive drawings and photographs. The great medieval barn is now a visitor and conservation centre where much of the Knole collections are treated.

1887 Fire

Restored medieval barn, now a visitor and conservation centre

INSPIRED BY KNOLE

The renovation and building programme at Knole was the largest conservation project in the National Trust, and was supported by a generous grant from the National Lottery Heritage Fund. This project was launched in an effort to rescue the house and its collections, as both were falling into a seriously poor state of repair. As part of 'Inspired by Knole' the aim of the archaeological project was threefold: to record and analyse those parts of the property impacted by the current work programme, to engage staff, visitors and volunteers alike with the archaeology of Knole, and to disseminate the results of the archaeological work through a wide variety of different methods.

A wealth of discoveries has included ritual protection marks engraved into wood and stone, extensive graffiti, evidence of historic fire damage, a hidden message in a bottle and forgotten seventeenth-century letters which had slipped beneath the floorboards. In many places the medieval fabric of the house, hidden by later changes, has been revealed including windows and doorways blocked behind panelling as the house was reconfigured. The project has also seen new areas of the house opened to the public for the first time including the carefully restored Gatehouse Tower. Some of the attic and domestic areas of the house have been opened to guided tours, presenting an atmospheric contrast to the grand Showrooms.

17th century letter

Eastern range roof stripped of tiles

The Church's location, close to the roadside, and its given name of St Nicholas, the patron saint of travellers, are both indicators that some kind of wayside chapel probably existed here as far back as the Saxon period. This would have been primarily for the benefit of drovers involved in transhumance, moving animals from one place to the next. The first written evidence for a church building of any kind lies in the 'Textus Roffensis', compiled under the direction of Bishop Ernulf of Rochester around 1120. We do not know what this 12th century building looked like. However, as the settlement of Sevenoaks grew, local ragstone would have been used to provide a more substantial building. This probably happened around 1257 when Henry de Gand was Rector as the bases of the pillars in the nave date from this time. Henry de Gand also obtained permission from the Archbishop of Canterbury Boniface to establish a chantry in the Church where prayers were said for the souls of the departed. Further building took place in the 15th century. Among other things, the 90 ft Tower was built. The 15th century re-building is normally attributed to the Archbishop of Canterbury, Thomas Bourchier, who bought Knole in 1456. Since then, the interior of St Nicholas Church has been much altered. However, the exterior remains largely as today.

St Nicholas Church

St Nicholas Church Tower

St Nicholas Church had a separate Rector and Vicar as the former could often be non-resident in the parish. The most notable absentee Rector was the famous preacher and metaphysical English poet John Donne, who held the position of Rector of St Nicholas from 1616 until his death in 1631 but only preached once at the Church in July 1617. It was during the period of the Curteis dynasty who held the 'advowson' – the right to appoint clergy for St Nicholas Church - for nearly 200 years (1716-1907) that the posts of Rector and Vicar were merged in 1750. The Rev Dr. Thomas Curteis was also responsible for installing today's peal of eight bells in 1769-71. The original 'six bells' live on today in nearby Six Bells Lane which was named after them.

The next major event to the Church's architecture came in the early 19th century. While there were chapels at Knole and Bradbourne, the Parish Church of St Nicholas was still required to serve the whole Sevenoaks community (1801 census 2,640) but seating was extremely limited. The Church was also both damp and gloomy inside. A survey in 1810 found in addition that the Church's roof required repair and the Tower was close to collapse. The cost of renovation was estimated to be £10,000 – a huge sum - such that it required a private Act of Parliament to levy a special rate on all landowners. The reconstruction, carried out by the distinguished architect S P Cockerell, from 1811-14, led to significant changes. The Tower was strengthened, the walls of the nave were raised with new clerestory windows, roof and clock. The result was a much lighter interior and a Church that could now seat at least one quarter of the Sevenoaks population.

Many monuments can be found inside the church, including the Amherst memorial chapel which was installed where the former Chantry Chapel had been sited. Most memorial plaques relate to the great Sevenoaks families of the day such as Lambarde, Camden, Boswell and Farnaby, or to individuals such as Dr Thomas Fuller, an eminent physician who lived at The Red House. The most recent change to the Church involved excavating under it. Completed in 1995, the construction of an 'Undercroft' has provided much needed space for activities on site, including a range of assembly rooms, a cafe and bookshop.

Amherst Chapel, formerly the Chantry Chapel

In 1810, the Rector purchased land from the next-door Chantry farm to provide an extended graveyard or cemetery. Although it is now closed to visitors, except with permission from the Church, it holds many interesting memorials, including the graves of both of Charles Dickens's daughters 'Kate' and 'Mamie'.

Grave of Charles Dickins's eldest daughter Mary
'Mamie' Dickens (1838-96)

Grade II* Listed Chantry House, formerly known as The Chantry

Little is known of how the Reformation affected Sevenoaks locally. However, records exist to show that it did affect the Chantry in Sevenoaks which had been established by Henry de Gand in 1257. Henry VIII obtained authority from Parliament in 1546 to suppress the Chantries in England. The Sevenoaks Chantry was duly abolished two years later in 1548 and the house and land where the Chantry priest lived was sold.

The present Grade II* Listed Chantry House was built in the late 17th century on the site of the earlier Chantry building. A datestone on one of the garden walls carries the inscription 1686. It is possible that the footings are original, as the cellars contain an apsidal space which may be the remnants of a medieval building. Built of red-brick, it has supporting wings on either side. These project to the roadside. A low screen wall with stone coping encloses a central paved courtyard. The house was greatly extended to the south in 1905 – a terracotta plaque records the date - by the architect J Compton-Hall using arts and crafts forms which imitate the materials and details of the main Chantry House. The Blue Pilgrims Fellowship, a missionary charity which was founded by Beatrice Hankey in 1902, appears to have occupied the buildings in the 20th century until The Beatrice Hankey Foundation sold the entire property in the 1970s.

SEVENOAKS SCHOOL

Sevenoaks School was endowed almost 600 years ago by William Sevenoke's Will of 1432. From humble beginnings, as a free lay school for the poor and probably with only one school room and one schoolmaster, Sevenoaks School is today a success story. With over 1,000 pupils, it is a major co-educational independent secondary school with a significant overseas contingent. History has it that William Sevenoke was an orphan, gaining his name from a combination of the Town where he was found and from his foster father, Sir William Romschedde, who owned a manor house near Riverhill. Like his contemporary, the infamous Richard (Dick) Whittington, Sevenoke found fame and fortune in London, eventually becoming Mayor of London in 1418. His desire to endow a 'Free' Grammar School in Sevenoaks is attributed to gratitude for his upbringing in the Town.

The School's initial income had been supplemented by a gift of 15 acres of land near Hollybush Lane in 1510, known as 'School Lands', from local townsfolk William Pett, Richard Blackboy and others. But it was Ralph Bosville, a successful lawyer with strong links to the Tudor Court, who helped ensure the little School's survival. Queen Elizabeth I visited him at his Bradbourne estate which Bosville had bought in 1555 and was persuaded to issue 'Letters Patent' in 1560 which provided new governance and a constitution for the School. She also granted the School the right to be known as the 'Queen Elizabeth's Grammar School'. In the 20th century, Sevenoaks School reverted to its founder's name.

SEVENOAKS SCHOOL

'Old School House' dated 1732

Constructed over a number of years, the 'Old School House' building on the High Street was finally completed in 1732. The original design was by the distinguished Palladian architect, the Earl of Burlington, but was subsequently altered, such that the finished design owed much to other architects, notably Lord Herbert and Roger Morris.

Built of squared Kentish ragstone blocks with galleting, the four-storeyed building has three central bays with wings on each side intended to be one story lower. However, in 1879, the architect of St Mary's Church Kippington, John Hooker, heightened the right side (to provide a dormitory) and upset the symmetry. It nonetheless remains an imposing building with a statue of William Sevenoke in its centre.

SEVENOAKS SCHOOL

Despite its royal connection and grand building, the School continued to struggle for survival until the 20th century when two important benefactors in particular - Francis Swanzy and Charles Plumptre Johnson - helped set it on the path to its current success. Their generous bequests enabled the School to expand significantly. It now has a 100-acre campus including seven boarding houses, a state-of-the-art Science and Technology Centre, a Sixth Form Global Study Centre, an award-winning performing arts centre, and the Sennocke Centre for PE and Sport. These buildings consist of a diverse mix of architectural styles ranging from the 18th century to the present day.

18th century Manor House in High Street, originally built as a Dower House for Knole, acquired by School in 1946.

19th century Johnson's Boarding House in Oak Lane, a gift from C P Johnson in 1927.

SEVENOAKS PLACE ALMSHOUSES

Grade II* Listed Almshouses to the left of the 'Old School House' building

For almost 1,000 years, charitable Almshouses in England have played a key role in providing retirement homes for the poor. William Sevenoke's Will of 1432 also provided for Almshouses: *"Twenty Men or Women, I will to dwell in the Mansion houses within the said Town of Sennocke."* The responsibility for both School and Almshouses was given initially to the nearby St Nicholas Parish Church and, a century later, to a Corporation of two Wardens and four Assistants. When Sevenoaks School was re-built in its present form (1728-1732), the Almshouses were re-built as well in similar style and colouring. They consist of two long wings. Each was originally constructed of 16 dwellings, on either side of the 'Old School House' which is located in the centre well back from the road. In 1877, a 15 strong Board of Governors took over responsibility for both School and Almshouses. By 1967, the task of governing both proved too cumbersome and a separate body of trustees was established to administer the Almshouses. The historic links with the Parish Church and School have however been maintained by including the Rector of St Nicholas and four of the School's Governors on the Board of Trustees.

The Almshouses proved a success from the outset. Applicants needed to be of good character and to have been resident in the town for at least 12 years. Once admitted, they were given a small allowance and required to attend St Nicholas Church. Detailed account books exist from the late 16th century. They give an insight into daily life at that time, including medical care. Incidents are recorded of drunkenness and disorderly behaviour but these seem to have been relatively rare. In the 19th century, overcrowding, shown in census returns, seems to have been a constant problem. In 1851, a total of 58 people for the 32 dwellings was recorded including some grandchildren. Local benefactors have helped to supplement the Almshouses' income. In 1921, the Rev Thompson of Kippington Church gave six cottages in nearby Oak Square to help provide income for the residents. Three of these remain, now leased to Sevenoaks School. More recently, the accommodation has been enlarged, reducing the overall number of Almshouses to 16. They have also been extensively refurbished, including bathroom facilities and modern kitchens.

Heritage Buildings in the Town Centre

Geraldine Tucker, Keith Wade & Veronica Coath

"In the relatively short stretch before it [the High Street] divides and descends into the valley, there are more worthwhile buildings than in almost any other street in the county." Pevsner's Architectural Guide 'Kent: West and the Weald' by John Newman. Unusually for an English town, Sevenoaks is built on a hill-top. Its most distinctive feature is its Y shape. From the early medieval period onwards, this small market town benefitted from its placement on the two main roads from London and Dartford, meeting at the top of the town, and continuing as a single road to Tonbridge and onwards to the coast. Today, only remnants of the Town's medieval buildings survive, notably in 'The Shambles'. Late medieval and Tudor structures include 'The Old Post Office' and the 'Reeve's House'.

Sevenoaks was given a welcome boost by the discovery of the 'Chalybeate Spring' by the 3rd Baron North in 1606. Thought to have medicinal properties, this natural spring led to the rapid growth of Tunbridge Wells, including royal patronage. It also helped Sevenoaks to prosper, as the town was conveniently placed on the coaching road between London and the Wells. Fine 17th century houses such as 'The Red House' were built in this period. More humble dwellings are found in the 18th and 19th century cottages in Six Bells Lane. 'Oak End' began life as two 18th century workers' dwellings but was transformed in the 19th century into a distinguished building. The chapter ends with the 19th century stories of the 'Old Market House' in the High Street and the former Lady Boswell's School building in London Road.

In the 13th century, the Sevenoaks market became established within the triangle bounded by the High Street on the east, London Road on the west, and Bank Street on the north. Medieval markets were often triangular, as this was thought to be the fairest way to give traders equal opportunities. The Shambles lay at the heart of this area and was, importantly, the place where the town's butchers and fishmongers

carried out their trade. It became easier for stallholders to leave their stalls in situ for the weekly market which soon turned into permanent shop premises initially built of timber with thatched roofs. The standings for the market stalls were separated by a network of intersecting alleyways with openings to the High Street and the London Road, many still existing today. From a narrow selling point at the front, buildings tended to develop backwards towards the inner centre of The Shambles. Most had substantial cellars, built for storage of goods.

Remnants of these medieval market premises still exist. Dorset Street, laid out at the end of the 16th century, has a plaque bearing the date 1605 near the narrow entrance to the Shambles. The image of the King's head above the

date was added in the 19th century by a former owner of the building. The lane contains a building, mainly timber framed, with crown post truss and collar purlin dating from 1450.

The Shambles area was highly unsanitary even up to the late 19th century. With no proper drainage, blood from animal carcasses as well as general rubbish and even sewage ran onto the High Street. By this time labourers from the Knole estate were also living there, in huts, in cramped conditions, and walking to work via Webbs Alley. Competition, particularly from Tonbridge, increased with the new rail links and the importance of The Shambles as a market diminished. Now only painted murals in The Shambles square show the scenes of its former market activities.

THE OLD POST OFFICE

The Old Post Office in 1901

Numbers 13, 15 and 17 in the Upper High Street date from the early part of the 15th century and were originally built as one. Initially it may have been the town house of one of the outlying manors. Together, they are a remarkable example of the style of residences that were being constructed at that time as the market town of Sevenoaks expanded, and of their subsequent varied use. At no.13, The Old Post Office has for many years served as the tuck-shop of Sevenoaks School and at one time was an inn, probably the Three Cats (despite a strong tradition that the Old House at no.18 was the inn of that name).

Around 1510, the Frith family moved from Westerham to Sevenoaks, where Richard Frith became innkeeper of the Three Cats. Here his son John lived as a young boy, attending Sevenoaks School. He was burned at the stake at Smithfield on 4th July 1533 after being found guilty of heresy, a martyr to the Protestant cause – as, three years later, was William Tyndale, who had deeply influenced Frith's beliefs. (One week after Frith's execution, Henry VIII was excommunicated).

Huge oak beams frame the ancient Grade II* building on its Kentish ragstone foundations, with its upper floors faced with hanging tiles. The shop front bays of no.13 are 19th century. Some of the original medieval vertical framing is exposed on the ground floor of no.15, beneath its large projecting central gable with its fish-scale tiles. The hanging wooden counters below the windows recall its life also as a shop, quite possibly selling produce from the adjacent Chantry and Rectory Farms. For a while in the 20th century, refreshments could be obtained from The Chantry Cottage Tea Rooms no. 17. Both nos. 15 and 17 are now private houses.

THE REEVE'S HOUSE

Situated on the junction of the High Street and Rockdale Road, this striking Grade II Listed building dating back over 500 years is thought to have been the home and office of the Archbishop's Reeve. A Reeve, or agent, was usually a resident local senior official with administrative responsibilities. Among other things, the Reeve would have enforced the rights of the Archbishop's manor of Otford in the Sevenoaks area. He would have collected any local taxes and rents owed to the Archbishop, overseen works that needed to be carried out and sorted out local disputes, all on behalf of the Archbishop.

The architectural historian John Newman describes the Reeves House as a large late medieval hall house of Wealden type. Inside, it has a fine early 16th century chimneypiece on which the coats of arms of Archbishop Chichele (1414-1443) and Archbishop Warham (1502-1532) are engraved in the spandrels of the fireplace's decorative stone surround. Warham may well have re-built part or all of the Reeves House in the early 16th century on the site of an older building erected by his predecessor Chichele. Three 18th century sash windows distinguish the front. However, the building's most noticeable feature is its 19th century red pattern fish-scale tile hanging.

The shop fronts were also added in the 19th century. W Loveland is thought to have had a leather business there in the mid-19th century. On his death around 1870, his assistant James Outram took over the leather business. He also opened a saddlery in the premises in 1880. Outram's business thrived, diversifying in the 20th century into sports and travel goods. It closed only in 2001, since when it has been a restaurant.

The Red House stands on the site of an original dwelling built in the early 17th century and was bought by Matthew Couchman in 1631. This dwelling was completely rebuilt for the Couchman family in 1686. Save for the insertion of the 18th century doorcase, the Red House's main exterior remains largely unchanged. In Pevsner's 'Kent: West and the Weald', John Newman calls The Red House *"the finest house in the street"*, representing the late 17th century ideal. The building has seven bays with the heavy cornice of the large hipped roof possessing highly decorated carved brackets.

It is also one of the Town centre's most interesting buildings historically, linked as it is with the famous pharmacist Dr Thomas Fuller and also the family of the novelist Jane Austen. Dr Fuller bought The Red House in 1688 and remained there until his death in 1734. He is most famous for his book on prescriptions. He claimed to have made a personal trial of every medicine before he prescribed it for his patients. Such prescriptions regularly involved live millipedes and woodlice, the flesh of burnt mice, beetles, earthworms, live crayfish and crab's claws. Dr Fuller also extolled the excellence of beer and, ahead of his time, warned of the risks of tobacco smoking. In 1743, the local solicitor Francis Austen purchased The Red House. Jane Austen visited her great-uncle here in July 1788 when she was 12 years old and stayed for about a month. Although leased to others - it was for a short while a school - The Red House remained in the Austen family until 1913. It has been occupied since 1936 by solicitors Knocker & Foskett.

"Who has not trodden the steep and stony path bearing this name, and marvelled at the fancy which led some ancient landowner to pitch his humble tenements in such a break-neck spot?" So enquires Frank Richards about this *"very interesting relic of old Sevenoaks"* in his 1901 book "Old Sevenoaks". This picturesque lane off the Upper High Street is certainly worthy of sight and study: a vivid illustration of by-gone Sevenoaks – a jumble of alleys and footways off the two main streets, leading to small courtyards and gardens.

White-painted and weather-boarded 18th century and early 19th century cottages line the cobbled and York Stone lane as it descends to the sharp left turn into Rectory Lane at the bottom – where in front of no. 16 can be seen the water pump, in public use until piped water arrived in the second part of the 1800s. An ancient buttressed ragstone wall flanks the north side. Hidden in a courtyard behind nos. 31-37 High Street is the 19th century old bakery. A turn of the head towards the street brings to view a remarkable catslide roof.

No. 37 High Street at the lane's head, now a coffee shop, was once the Six Bells Alehouse: its name – and hence the lane alongside - taken from the original six bells of St Nicholas' church. These were melted down and new metal added in 1769 to make today's peal of eight. For a time in the mid-19th century the lower part of the pathway after the bend was called Parsonage Lane before reverting to its original name.

Nos. 31-37, with their low overhanging jetty, were originally a single house. The four gables of this Grade II 16th century building were added c1860 and the timber-framing concealed by render and weatherboard. The awkward bend in the High Street is known locally as Raley's Corner, after the baker and pastry cook who traded there in the 1930s.

This drawing by local artist William Knight (1812-1878) shows nos. 31-37 High Street before the gables were added.

To the north of the lane are the brick-walled Upper High Street Gardens, one time fields overlooking meadows. Miss Joan Constant of The Old House opposite gifted this haven from the passing traffic to the Council in 1949 as a permanent public garden.

In the Sevenoaks Library is this interesting curiosity: an 1813 bill from Richard Crow, solicitor, to Messrs Hooper and Luckhurst for £55, 5s and 4d *"for frustrating the attempt to stop up Six Bells Lane"*. It seems that for some reason, the Justices of the Peace had issued an order removing the public right of way through the lane. In robust response, a Plan of Opposition was put into action. The 5-page invoice records in meticulous detail the expenses incurred from October 1811 to April 1813, including the costs of legal and agents' fees, attending meetings, perusing papers and writing letters. The bill was settled in December 1814 – and, it would appear, the plan was a success, enabling us all to scroll back through time in this quiet secluded spot.

Known locally as the 'Old Market House', this Grade II Listed neo-classical building dating from 1842 occupies a commanding position on an island site in the centre of the High Street. It replaced an unusual octagonal building of timber and tile with lattice working, built before 1554, which was enclosed at the top and open below, standing on timber columns on stone foundations. In the past, it was used as the venue for the Town's medieval manor courts. Rebels from Sir Thomas Wyatt's abortive rebellion in 1554 were tried at Sevenoaks Market House and executed on Gallows Common. The Sevenoaks Advertiser records the upper part's complete re-build in 1842, noting that it had also now been enclosed with a substantial iron palisading and entrance gate.

Both its use as a County Court and a Corn Market declined from the 1860s when a new police station was built and the rail links provided other venues for the corn market. In 1896, Henry Swaffield made it largely into the building we see today. He re-faced the exterior, refurbished the whole and gave it to the YMCA in 1900 as a reading room and social centre. When its upkeep proved too expensive for the YMCA, the Sevenoaks Urban District Council took over the lease and used it as a Public Library until the new Library was built in The Drive in 1905. The Old Market House became a Technical Institute in 1905 but that use was redundant by the 1920s. The building was converted into public conveniences in 1924 with a caretaker's flat above, known colloquially as 'Skinner's Palace' after the councillor who had proposed the idea. In 1979 it was sold and became commercial premises. The 1977 Jubilee clock on the exterior was installed by the Sevenoaks Town Council.

Even long-time residents of Sevenoaks may struggle to identify this distinguished building. It lies at the southern end of the Upper High Street. Its beginnings were humble: originally two

18th century timbered buildings, described as *"two messuages or tenements"* when they were bought in 1843 by a Captain Nepean. As part of the Sevenoaks Park estate, they were probably workers' cottages. Nepean converted them into one property, adding a large stone-built extension to the rear and remodelling the front in the stucco-Gothic manner. According to Jane Edwards (1868), this *"quaint-looking"* house originally faced west. As she recounts, an old lady named Mrs Blancho lived there before it was converted: she was infirm and could not use the stairs - so she had a square cut out of her bedroom floor and a "sort of chair" made for her to sit on, with pulleys to draw her up and down.

The view (below) of the stone extension from the garden provides a stark comparison with the front. Similarly the elegant Georgian-style interior at the rear contrasts with the front rooms with their exposed timbers and ancient fireplace. The ornamental cast-iron railings are 19th century.

The rear

The building as it appears now, with its dark brick frontage and tile-hung projecting porch.

Further modifications were made in the 20th century to the design of Arts and Crafts architects Baillie Scott and Beresford: c1930 the stucco was removed (together with various "frills" and "aberrations") to reveal the brickwork. Once more it became (as now) two properties by closing off the servants' quarters. In the drive beside Little Oak End can still be seen the cover of a large turntable used for coaches. The rare photograph above, discovered in the archives of Sevenoaks Library, reveals the building before that restoration. The Park Grange lodge built c1869 is not shown so it is possible that it was taken shortly after the mid-19th century changes.

In 1815, Sevenoaks had two charitable schools: the Queen Elizabeth's Grammar School (Sevenoaks School) and Lady Boswell's School, the latter named after its founder Lady Margaret Bosville (Boswell) (1604-1692) whose memorial is in St Nicholas Church. Lady Margaret, a great benefactress of Sevenoaks, inherited the Bradbourne lands from her father Sir Ralph Bosville. The Bosvilles had entertained Queen Elizabeth I at Bradbourne, securing a grant of 'Letters Patent' to Sevenoaks School as well as the Queen's agreement to Sevenoaks School's use of her name. Lady Margaret continued the process of helping education in Sevenoaks. In her will, she left an endowment to educate 12 poor scholars in the Town as well as two scholarships for Sevenoaks School pupils to Jesus College, Cambridge. No building seems to have been erected at that stage. The schoolmaster appointed by the Trustees taught his pupils in his own house which was probably attached in some way to Sevenoaks School. By 1815, the trustees, including Lord Amherst and Multon Lambard as well as Henry Thomas Lane of Bradbourne, decided that a school building was necessary. Buying land from the nearby 'Black Boy' garden, they commissioned an upcoming young architect, Charles Robert Cockerell, to build this Church of England aided primary school. From the beginning, it had close links to the Sevenoaks Parish Church, St Nicholas.

Cockerell later became a distinguished architect but the Grade II Listed Lady Boswell's School was his first building. Of squared Kentish ragstone, it consists of a three-bay block under a pediment carved with an armorial display by J C F Rossi. The 1818 date remains clearly visible on the upper exterior. Lady Boswell's School remained here until 1972 when it moved to a new purpose-built building in Plymouth Drive. The building then became the Sevenoaks Job Centre and latterly a restaurant.

Legacy of the Great Estates
Some remaining buildings and features

Elizabeth Purves

Sevenoaks used to be surrounded by huge estates. The major ones being Knole, Wildernesse, Montreal and Bradbourne, as shown on Hasted's map of Codsheath from the late 18th century.

Knole with its great house and park extended to almost 1,000 acres. Bradbourne estate of over 1,200 acres covered most of the northern part of Sevenoaks in the Sixteenth century. Wildernesse at one time extended to over 760 acres in Seal and Sevenoaks whilst Montreal estate stretched from Riverhead, Bessels Green, Kippington and Sundridge to Ide Hill, comprising of some 2,500 acres in the 1930s.

These large estates were owned by the landed gentry who lived in mansions they built on their land, and employed numerous people.

The Palladian style house of Montreal, built by General, later Lord, Jeffrey Amherst after he returned victorious from Canada in 1764 was huge. It had 27 bedrooms and seven large reception rooms. The Census of 1871 records that there were 23 servants living in the house. The 4th Earl of Amherst sold up before his death in 1926. The house was demolished in 1936 and much of the land sold for housing.

Amherst Obelisk

In the grounds of the estate, Amherst erected an obelisk in c.1764 to commemorate the reunion with his brothers after victory in Canada. The Kentish ragstone obelisk, on land adjoining the garden of 81 Montreal Park, is Grade II Listed. On the four marble panels there is an inscription recording Amherst's victories.

Also in the grounds of Montreal estate is a Grade II Listed summerhouse. The late 18th century gazebo had two arched openings, facing both east and west with a dividing wall between, so that the Amhersts could sit either side, depending upon the weather. It is now much decayed and has had its pediment removed.

Montreal Summerhouse

Several Montreal lodges survived after the great house was demolished.

The early 19th century octagonal Montreal Lodge, in what is now Lyndhurst Drive, is Grade II Listed. It was used as a sales office when William Fasey bought Montreal land for housing in 1933.

Montreal Lodge

Close to Montreal Lodge is a Grade II Listed gate house, Amherst Cottage, on the London Road.

Amherst Cottage

Another lodge, Amherst Lodge, is on the south side of Westerham Road in Bessels Green. The Amherst Crest is prominent on the façade.

Amherst Lodge

Amherst Lodge Crest

WILDERNESSE ESTATE

The Grade II Listed Wildernesse House, bought by the Camdens in 1705, and later enlarged by Lord Hillingdon, was another vast mansion.

The third Lord Hillingdon sold the estate during the 1920s. Some of the land was bought for large houses on substantial plots forming the present Wildernesse Estate, and some by Sevenoaks Urban District Council for social housing to form the Hillingdon estate.

Wildernesse House

The main drive to the house was the present Wildernesse Avenue. To commemorate the visit of the Duke of Wellington in 1815 just before the Battle of Waterloo, Lord Camden planted a great avenue of double rows of limes.

Waterloo Limes

Five of the lodges for Wildernesse still exist, two within Sevenoaks Town boundary. The single storey Avenue Lodge, in Seal Hollow Road built in 1803, marked the western entrance of the drive to the House. A second single storey lodge, Hillingdon Lodge, near Sevenoaks Hospital, was built by Lord Camden at the far end of a new drive along what is now Hillingdon Avenue. The new drive was built to avoid boggy land at Millpond Wood. Both lodges have the Camden crest, an elephant's head, on their walls.

Camden Crest   Hillingdon Lodge in 1908

Avenue Lodge in 1921

The eccentric Francis Crawshay who owned coal mines and iron foundries in Wales bought the Bradbourne estate in 1867, and erected some huge monoliths and Druidic circles within the grounds. One of these monoliths was moved from Robyns Way in 2003 to the entrance of the Bradbourne Lakes. Another, a tall Doric column of red Cornish granite is Grade II Listed and still in its original position in the back garden of 5 Pontoise Close. The column formed the centre piece of a Druidical circle, some of the remnants of which remain in other nearby gardens.

Monolith at entrance to Bradbourne Lakes

Monolith in the garden of 5 Pontoise Close

Bradbourne Lakes

When Bradbourne Hall was sold and demolished in 1927, land was bought by Ideal Homes who built the houses and bungalows of the Bradbourne Lakes estate. The old ornamental lakes, laid out by Henry Bosville in the mid 18th century, were bought by Sevenoaks Urban District Council to make a seven acre public park.

Few estate buildings remain. There is a lodge in Betenson Avenue, the Grade II Listed Clock House in Clock House Lane and Bottle Cottages in Bradbourne Vale Road. The attractive Bottle Cottages, built before 1840, have bottle glass in decorative panels, hence the name.

Bradbourne Lodge

Bottle Cottages

The Clock House was built in the mid 18th century as a pair of cottages for estate workers. It was disguised to look like a small gothic chapel, a trompe d'oeil, which could be seen from Bradbourne House. The timber belvedere with the clock on top of the stone tower, may well have been added by Francis Crawshay.

The Clock House   Clock Mechanism

When William James Thompson bought the Kippington Estate in 1865, it consisted of some 268 acres of parkland. In the centre was Kippington House, with lodges at either end of the drive. At the northern end is Beech Lodge, and at the southern end, the Grade II Listed Kippington Lodge.

Kippington House

Beech Lodge

Kippington Lodge in the late 19th century

A third lodge is at the entrance of Kippington Court. Originally built by Thompson as a new gate house for Kippington Park, this Grade II Listed lodge became the lodge for Kippington Court.

Kippington Court Lodge in 1938

Farms

Keith Wade

Bethlehem Farm in 1800

From the earliest settlements until Victorian times Sevenoaks' landscape was essentially agricultural. For 700 years or more, farms were a predominant feature of not just the countryside but the town itself, cultivated in medieval times by tenants paying rent and taxes to the Archbishop's Manor of Otford. By the age of the Tudors, to the north was a crescent of farms, including Chevening, Dryhill, Chipstead and Morants. In a ring around the town were Dibden, Kippington, Brittains, Greatness, Bradbourne, Blackhall, Rumstead, Panthurst, Wickhurst, and of course Knole. Nearer the centre stood Sevenoaks Park Farm (where Park Grange is now), St Nicholas' Glebe (Rectory Farm), Lock's Bottom, Hillborough, and the farm later to be known as Bligh's. The Kent Historic Environment Record includes 25 farmsteads within the town, including Cross Keys, Dransfield (Ashgrove), Fig Street, Shangden, St John's and Wildernesse.

Many farms developed into grand estates, passing from Church to Crown, thence to the noble and favoured, and onward to the nouveaux riches, their fields leased to numerous tenants over the centuries. New estates such as Montreal emerged as well as smaller holdings including Covell's, west of London Road.

Most farms of any size were mixed arable and pastoral, with tenants and landowners growing crops, holding livestock and coppicing woodland for their own use or commercial gain. Some had permanent footholds around Sevenoaks market-place. Following their introduction at the end of the 15th century, hops became a major crop and oast-houses a distinctive feature of the landscape. With the decline of agricultural profits and the mounting of debts, and the rapid expansion of Sevenoaks after the coming of the railways, most buildings were demolished or converted to other uses and land sold for development. For example with the opening of Tubs Hill station in 1868, land in Covell's Farm was sacrificed to make way for new houses and roads – and with it was lost the weather-boarded Knotts smock windmill, the last in town.

However many of the farms and fields of the past are recalled in the street-names of Sevenoaks. And several significant buildings and traces do survive as an important legacy of those former times – although their origins are not always evident to the undiscerning eye.

The prominent Grade II Listed building in the High Street, now the Oak Tavern and Taphouse, is all that remains of Bligh's Farm. Its restored front conceals a 16th century timber-framed farm-house. It is possible that the original 13th century farm was the home-farm of the Archbishop of Canterbury's holding in Sevenoaks, with a vineyard to the north. In 1654 for £1,010 the London Parish of St Botolph without Bishopsgate acquired the farm from Sir Ralph Bosville of Bradbourne, together with barn, stables and land totalling 74½ acres, including a hop-garden.

By 1800 it had become known as Bethlehem or "Bedlam" Farm. (The claim that it was once a country outpost of London's Bethlehem Hospital is an urban myth). Samuel Bligh acquired the lease in 1852, established a brewery and turned rooms into lodgings – the first Bligh's Hotel. Around 1900 land was sold and farm buildings demolished to make way for Pembroke Road. Farm operations ceased in 1919, and the oasts, barns and dairy were pulled down as derelict.

The entrance to Bligh's Farm c1875

The hotel was restored in 1929 after itself being threatened with demolition. The campaign to save it was orchestrated by the Sevenoaks and District Housing and Town Planning Association - a forerunner of The Sevenoaks Society. In the 1950s and 1960s the hotel's King's Hall became a popular venue for top-flight pop groups and youngsters eager to dance the night away. The Beatles changed there when filming their Strawberry Fields video in Knole Park in 1967. Now after a chequered history it continues as a pub and home to a micro-brewery, and the fields (Bligh's Meadow) are a shopping centre.

PARK FARM

Park Grange, now owned by Sevenoaks School, sits on the site of the ancient farm in Sevenoaks Park, created c1500 on the southern edge of the town. Across the road was Gatiers, a smallholding going back to at least Elizabethan times. In 1654 Thomas

Lambarde, newly possessed of the Park, bought and did away with Gatiers' house and hop-gardens, and had the line of the road changed to its present form to provide a little more privacy. The print shows Park Place in 1818, the Palladian mansion that was home to the Lambardes until their departure in 1837 when Park Grange was erected in its stead.

BRITTAINS

Brittains Farmhouse

Rear view of Brittains Oasthouse

In the words of Sevenoaks District Council *"It is a pleasant surprise to find this enclave of historic tranquillity so close to the built fringes of the town"*. The Grade II Listed ragstone farmhouse was built by Sir Thomas Farnaby in 1751, the oast a year earlier. The dates and Farnaby's initials are written on plaques in both. The large barn is reputed to date from the 15th century.

Brittains Farm is first recorded in 1274 but its origins may be earlier. For eight generations it was held on behalf of the Archbishop of Canterbury by the de Bruton family (hence the name). After Henry VIII "acquired" the estate from Cranmer, it eventually passed into the hands of Sir Ralph Bosville of Bradbourne, whose family owned it for about 200 years until bought in 1749 by Farnaby, who absorbed it into his Kippington estate. To pay off his considerable debts, in 1796/7 his son Sir Charles Farnaby-Radcliffe (the 3rd Baronet) sold the whole estate to Francis Motley Austen (a cousin of Jane). A succession of tenant farmers grew hops and tended livestock. Brittains survived the 1936 break-up of the Kippington and Montreal estates, both the farmhouse and oasthouse continuing in private ownership. Jersey dairy cows were still kept at Brittains until the 1960s.

Brittains' ancient barn

BRADBOURNE FARMHOUSE

A roof tile showing the date of the building

The impressive Grade II* farmhouse on the north of Bradbourne Vale Road, described in Pevsner's Guide as *"a delightful example"* of its type, was built in 1702 for Charles Farnaby of Kippington (the 1st Baronet). The farm was one of several in the "Little Park of Otford" (part of the manor of Otford and originally a deer park), each in the centre of a parcel of land called a "yoke". His grandfather, the first Thomas Farnaby, the distinguished Classical scholar and school-master, had acquired the lease in 1645. The park was separate from the Bradbourne estate to the south, owned by the Bosvilles from the 16th to mid 18th century, which had its own farm. The Grade II Listed converted barn opposite is also 18th century. The farm-lands were extensive, and as recently as 1935 cornfields stretched north of the A25 and an Elizabethan barn stood where Knole Academy is sited.

An early 20thC postcard

The front and sides of the original double-pile house, with its hipped tiled roof, are largely unaltered. What appears from the front as a fashionable design of the time turns into a vernacular building at the rear. The two classical door-cases are probably late 18th century insertions.

Clenches Farm was established by Francis Motley Austen as a Home Farm after his purchase of the Kippington estate. A 1797 conveyance map indicates that an isolated barn surrounded by fields ("Clinches") was on the site before then. This surviving six-bay timber-framed Grade II Listed 18th century barn is typical of its kind, and the south end wall incorporates Kentish ragstone from an earlier building. From the 1890s to 2004, the farm was used for dairy operations, and the barn became a bottling plant. Other farm buildings were subsequently demolished to make way for the present housing development. The imposing redbrick Clenches Farm House (1889) was originally the dairy manager's house.

The barn before conversion

Clenches Farm from the OS map of 1895

The ancient manor of Blackhall goes back to at least the 13th century and may predate Knole and Wildernesse. As elsewhere in town it was for a period in the hands of the Bosvilles. In the late 18th century part was acquired by the Dorsets of Knole, and in 1826 the estate was divided between Knole and the Camdens of Wildernesse, Blackhall Lane being the dividing line. The original manor was extensive, with holdings in Sevenoaks and beyond. But the farm complex that formed part of the Lord of the Manor's demesne* can still be seen, now converted into private dwellings, between Blackhall Lane and the wall of Knole Park.

The oldest part of Blackhall House (locally listed) dates back to c1600 and is believed to be on the site of the original farmhouse. Little Blackhall is a Grade II restored 16th or 17th century cottage. Blackhall Barns was originally an 18th century outfarm. The picture shows the view of the granary and oast from the fields, a welcome oasis of calm on the edge of the town.

To the west, on lands on the park side of the Hole in the Wall entrance to Knole, lay **LOCK'S BOTTOM FARM**, the property of the Locke family until sold by Nicholas Locke c 1598. He was a governor of Sevenoaks School, and according to Dr Gordon Ward, *"a most respectable yeoman"*.

*lands reserved for his own use

The double square oasts of Greatness still stand sadly and incongruously, minus their cowls, amidst the dust and noise of the sand quarry.

Greatness Farm in its final years in the 1950s – and now.

For decades families flocked to Greatness to pick the hops; whilst the menfolk no doubt placed bets on the outcome of races at the Sevenoaks racecourse. (The inaugural 2-day meeting was held in April 1866 "on Mr R Russell's farm at Greatness Park". Eight years later HRH Prince Arthur, son of Queen Victoria, was present to celebrate his winnings). Hopping continued until the 1960s.

Two scenes from 1919: potato fields and "Grandstand Cottage"

Dibden Farm in 1938. Today the A21 thunders close by.

The first recorded date of a settlement at Dibden is 1270. The Grade II 16th century farmhouse may have been a small hall-house, and, situated on the original Rye Road, at one time a beer-house. From Tudor times it was part of the Kippington Estate.

ST NICHOLAS' GLEBE (RECTORY FARM)

Although the farm and its buildings have gone, the view from Rectory Lane remains much the same today.

A glebe is land, sometimes containing a farm, which was assigned by the church to support the priest, in addition to the rectory and grounds. In 1810 the churchyard of St Nicholas was extended, and the rector, the Reverend TS Curteis, gave up land where his barn and stables stood, on condition that they be rebuilt elsewhere. The present farmhouse is 20th century, erected on the site of the former building. In 1931, the Laurie family of Rockdale bought much of the glebe land; in 1938 they sold the farm, which was then demolished.

CHANTRY FARM lay to the south of St Nicholas' cemetery, the farmlands being the endowment of the chantry established by the church in 1257. The farmhouse was on the site of the present late 17th century Chantry in the High Street.

In 1654 part of the lands of the ancient farm of Hillborough was owned by the Quaker, Nathaniel Owen, by trade a mercer. Secret meetings of Quakers were held in the fields, and by association the area became known as Quaker's Hall Farm (also called Stoneville Farm). Much of the land was sold for housing development in 1876.

The house, Quaker's Hall, was built by Thomas Hilder in 1760, close to the original farmhouse; a barn in the grounds provided timbers which can still be seen in the building in Bayham Road. Both the house (above) and the nearby 17th century framed Quaker's Hall Cottage are Grade II Listed.

For refusing to pay his tithes, in 1699 ten hundred-weights of hops worth £43 were sequestered from Owen, who like other Quakers was several times jailed for his beliefs.

Public Houses, Taverns and Inns

Keith Wade

The British "pub" is a unique institution, having evolved from a number of different drinking establishments: humble ale- and beer-houses, wine taverns, gin palaces and travellers' inns. In 1901, 60 pubs were recorded in the Sevenoaks area; there were 25 within the town's boundary in the 1950s - only eight remain open today. The closure of a public house is not just the loss of another drinking establishment – the town also loses a part of its heritage. Pubs are local institutions, many in Sevenoaks going back centuries, a vital part of the social and economic fabric of the town, and inextricably connected to its development.

A pub's name and sign may betray its early history, and people and events associated with it. The Rifleman, Black Boy, White Hart, and Chequers all have stories to tell – as did the Bat and Ball, Oddfellows and Foresters Arms, Railway and Bicycle, Vine Tavern, and much-lamented Farmers – all now gone along with many others.

Several of the pubs in the town occupy historic buildings, and are notable for their architecture, distinctive features, and connections to the past. Some hostelries, such as the 18th century Royal Oak and the Victorian Man of Kent (now housing), were purpose-built, to take advantage of location or to meet a local need. Others were originally a private dwelling, and over time began to offer beer, wine and/or spirits – and sometimes

accommodation too, as for example Bligh's Hotel, transformed from a 16th century farmhouse and now the Oak Tavern and Tap House.

Bligh's Hotel c 1905/10.
The building and its history are featured in the Farms chapter of this book.

THE LOCAL PUB

The variety of pubs reflects their origins as well as age, purpose and architecture. Some are grand and spacious, others small and unpretentious, such as the "local", the modern successor to the medieval ale-house. But as social habits change, and costs and taxes rise, many of these struggle to survive. However, although their numbers are much reduced, several in Sevenoaks continue to thrive and maintain the custom of serving the local community.

Bank Street c 1920, showing the 17th century Black Boy pub in the centre.

This traditional town pub in London Road possibly dates back to the early 18th century. A row of old cottages was demolished to make way for the original beer-house. It was remodelled in 1923, being reduced from three to two storeys and incorporating number 34, and has typical features of that period. Until about 50 years ago, it had three bars plus a

bottle-and-jug (take-away). With no maritime connection, the name probably derives from the religious significance of the anchor as a symbol of security and hope. Its long-serving landlord (a record 40 years in 2019) adds further justification to the pub's inclusion as a heritage asset.

The pub before the 1923 changes

This popular pub in Camden Road is the last example in Sevenoaks of a two-bar back-street local. It is the only remaining pub in the St John's and Hartslands area, which within living memory boasted ten. The pub takes its name from the soldiers who drank there. Shortly after war broke out with France in 1793, soldiers were billeted in barracks built on Gallows Common, and a beer-house was opened in one of the brick cottages used as officers' quarters. (Gallows Common is the name given to a triangle of land to the west of St John's Hill; it is said that public hangings there date back to at least 1554). The barracks were demolished in 1815 after the Battle of Waterloo so it is possible that this was when the soldiers' bar became a "public" house.

The Halfway House

This historic pub existed in the 18th century, and is one of the last independent free houses in Sevenoaks. The front part is a 19th century addition, most likely built to take advantage of the coming of the railway at Tubs Hill; but the timber-frame rear retains the structure and features of the original building. The name and its isolated position north of the town may indicate that it was originally a coaching inn positioned halfway between two turnpikes. (The first turnpike in Kent, from Riverhill to Tonbridge and Tunbridge Wells, was established by a 1709 Act of Parliament. A northern stretch, to Farnborough and on to London, came 40 years later). Still serving its purpose in providing refreshment for travellers, the pub is a popular stopping-off point for commuters as well as a convivial meeting-point for locals.

One of the oldest hostelries in Sevenoaks, the Grade II Black Boy in Bank Street is recorded as a "messuage" (dwelling with out-buildings) in 1637, although most of the present structure is late 18th century. Gabled buildings that used to exist in a yard to the rear were said by Historic England to be 16th century or 17th century. There are several suggestions as to the origin of its name, but it is most likely that the pub is so called after Richard Blackboy, a local landowner and benefactor in Tudor times. However it is not an uncommon name: the sign was often hung outside coffee houses and taverns in the 17th century. The pub once had extensive gardens extending to Bethlehem Farm; the first Lady Boswell's school (latterly a restaurant) was built in the grounds in 1818.

THE DORSET ARMS

Elizabeth Petley is recorded as the keeper of this ancient London Road establishment back in 1613, but it may be much older than that. Then it was the Bull – or Pied Bull (to distinguish it from the other Bull inns in town). A deed of 1670 refers to it as the "Earl of Dorset Arms", in honour of Thomas Sackville, Lord Treasurer, who was made the first earl in 1604, a year after becoming master of Knole. It too had considerable land with stables across the road off the "malodorous and pestilential" Brands Lane (now South Park). The present handsome structure dates from a rebuilding in 1887. After closing in 2006 it became a succession of restaurants and is currently the Cote Brasserie. Tradition has it that the doorway of the inn was the scene of the last stand against the forces of Jack Cade after the battle of Solefields in 1450.

Coaching and Post Inns

In their Georgian heyday, coaching inns enjoyed a steady trade in providing rest and refreshment for travellers in private carriages and public stage-coaches, as well as serving as staging-posts for the mail-coach. Most inns had stables and supplied fresh teams of horses. The advent of the railways heralded their decline as such, but many survive as pubs, restaurants or hotels. Sevenoaks was particularly favoured as being on the Rye Road from London to the coast, and also convenient for those destined for the waters at Tunbridge Wells. The four featured here are all Grade II. Other coaching inns in the centre of town were the Royal Crown, Rose and Crown, and Wheatsheaf.

The London Road frontage of the old Chequers Inn, showing the 18th century addition to the left.

THE CHEQUERS

The Chequers building in the High Street dates back to the 16th or early 17th century, but it's likely that there's been an inn here since the 12th century. For hundreds of years this area was the throbbing heart of Sevenoaks, hosting its market and twice-yearly fair. The Romans brought the sign of the chequers to Britain, to indicate that chess could be played in their *tabernae* (wine-bars). But the present name dates to 1707 and most probably refers to the chequer-board or cloth on the money-tables handling the market's transactions. It is said that convicted criminals were held in the inn's cellars, hanged from the nearby gallows and their

bodies thrown into the lime-pit which is now part of the pub. A famous 19th century stage-coach, the United Friends, started and terminated its journeys to London here.

Market Square c1865-70

As its appearance and location demonstrate, this was once the most prestigious inn in town. Kings and queens are said to have stayed here; the crest proudly asserts its royal connections and the doric columns its grandeur. A splendid old sign showed the future King Charles II hiding in an oak tree. Sadly now closed, its fate is at present uncertain. Originally the Black Bull and called the Royal Oak from at least 1785, it was refronted in its present local stone blocks c1820. It once had a long room projecting beyond the front which was used for balls and as officers' quarters in war-time. The Excelsior, still running in 1889, was one of the many stage- and mail-coaches that stopped here. (Its claim to be the premier inn would in fact have been disputed by the very grand and ancient Royal Crown, demolished in the 1930s. The STAG complex and the post office now occupy that site).

The Upper High Street showing the Royal Oak c 1870. The neighbouring Royal Oak Tap (now a private house) was once a forge as well as beer-house.

THE WHITE HART

The White Hart Inn on Sevenoaks Common probably first existed as a 17th century farmhouse-cum-hostelry catering for travellers on the long journey between London and the coast, and was well positioned to take advantage of Kent's first turnpike road of 1709. The building shows 18th century features and modifications, and more modern alterations; the stables became a garage, and more recently housing.

In 1393, King Richard II made it compulsory for alehouses to display signs. The white hart was Richard's heraldic badge, and the name was not surprisingly adopted by many inn-keepers to show loyalty. Later it became a generic term for a tavern. (At one time the White Hart, being opposite Knole Park and the home of the Sackvilles, was also called The Dorset Arms). Famous visitors included the artist CE Perugini and his wife Kate, the youngest daughter of Charles Dickens.

The main block of this historic building, latterly the Riverhead Harvester and now a steak-house, is 16th century; the jettied front with dragon beam at the angle may indicate it was originally a hall house. The south-side section is an 18th century extension. The name was taken in recognition of the Amherst family: the inn was on the edge of Sir Jeffrey Amherst's Montreal Estate created in 1764. In the 19th century the inn was an important posting-house on the London mail route, and the quality of its stables and horses was renowned. The old postcard shows the local Bobby riding by the hotel c1880.

Local Industry

Elizabeth Purves

Until the late 19th century, the town's major industry was agriculture.

When the railway arrived in 1862, it had a huge impact on the town. Now London was only an hour away on the train, people could live in Sevenoaks and commute daily. Speculative housing for these new residents led to a demand for bricks, rag stone, and sand for building, as well as services such as gas, electricity, water, shops and pubs. Much of this industry was located to the north of the town in the Greatness area.

The Bat and Ball Station

The first station to open in Sevenoaks was the Bat and Ball in 1862 when the line was extended from Swanley to Sevenoaks. The contractor who built the line, and the major shareholder of the newly formed Sevenoaks Railway Company, was Thomas Crampton. The nine mile line was originally single track but a year later had become double track. The line was officially opened on June 2nd 1862. A special train carrying the directors ran from Victoria to a temporary wooden station at the Bat and Ball whilst a permanent station was under construction.

The Grade II Listed station building which had been boarded up since 1992 has been re-furbished by Sevenoaks Town Council with the help of Lottery funding. The old booking hall has been meticulously restored,

and is now a room for community use. The original ticket office is to be used for a café and a new access to be made from platform 1 to the Community Centre.

Refurbished Booking Hall

Sorting coke at Sevenoaks Gasworks c 1903

The Sevenoaks Gas Company was established in 1838 to make and distribute gas from their works at the Gas House in Hartsland Road. The two main streets of the town had gas lights by 1840. In 1862, a rival gas company, Sevenoaks, Riverhead and Seal Gas Light and Coke Consumers Company was formed which led to the demise of the Hartslands gas works. In 1865 the new company found a site of one and three quarter acres in Cramptons Road to produce and store gas. By 1869, two gas holders had been erected. A total of four gas holders were built, the last one being in 1938. A tramway ran from the Bat and Ball Station up Cramptons Road into the gas works for bulk delivery of coal which was burned to produce the gas. With the discovery of gas in the North Sea, the local gas industry declined, as did the need for gas holders. Gas production ceased at the site in 1960.

The remaining two redundant gas holders were dismantled in 2018, and the land scheduled for housing.

Gas works in the 1950s

Gas holders in Cramptons Road in 2017

SAND AND GRAVEL QUARRIES

Sevenoaks Sand Quarry

The Greensand beds in the area were quarried for materials to use in the construction and building industries.

Sand and gravel was excavated from what is now the Wildlife Reserve from 1935 to 1980. The Harrison family formed an agreement in the 1970s with the Kent Sand and Ballast Company to develop the 180 acre site as a nature reserve.

Further east, 280 acres of the Sevenoaks Sand Quarry, owned by Tarmac and first quarried in 1928, stretches from east of the Bat and Ball station to Childsbridge Lane in Seal. Sand extraction will cease after 2030, when the site will be released by Tarmac. It is allocated in the Sevenoaks District Local Plan for 600 homes and a lake for leisure purposes.

The Ordnance Survey maps of 1869 and 1896 show numerous small quarries used to provide sand and gravel for local building needs.

Sevenoaks Sand Quarry works and old offices

BRICK FIELDS

The clamp where bricks were baked in Sevenoaks Brickworks .1968

Bricks were needed in large quantities for the construction of bridges, tunnels, signal boxes and stations for the railways, and also for speculative housing. Land at Greatness proved a good location for brick making with its sand, lime, chalk and brick earth or pug, all necessary to make bricks.

St Johns brickyard operated from what is now known as the Vestry Estate. Owned by the Norman family in 1828, it was bought by Thomas Crampton in 1861, an astute purchase, to supply the large number of bricks required for building the railway. A siding ran from the Bat and Ball station to the brick yard to transport materials. The brickyard closed in 1897 and was sold to Southwark Vestry for use as a rubbish dump.

To the west of Otford Road, near the Bat and Ball station, were large brickworks run by the builders Durtnells from the 1870 to 1938.

A further brickyard in Greatness was the Greatness Brickworks established in 1925. When Basil Jones bought the business in 1930 he changed the name to Sevenoaks Brickworks. At one time, these Sevenoaks Brickworks were producing 60 million bricks a year. Ibstock Brick bought the brickworks in 1980, but by 1991 they had closed due to the lack of demand for bricks. The site is now owned by Cory Environmental and used for landfill.

To the south of the town, the railway contractor John Jay, developed the Weald Brickworks to provide the large number of bricks needed for the Sevenoaks Tunnel, whilst in Dunton Green, William Thompson of Kippington set up the Dunton Green Brickworks in 1862.

WATER SUPPLY

Bore Hole in 1935

Originally the town's water supply was filled by springs, wells, pumps and ponds. During the construction of the Sevenoaks railway tunnel in 1864, the contractor, John Jay, hit underground water which flooded the works. Although this was a disaster for John Jay and bankrupted him, it provided a much needed source of clean water for the town. A shaft was sunk and pumps installed, with a storage reservoir built at Solefields by the Sevenoaks Waterworks Company, founded in 1871 by William Thompson, owner of Kippington estate. These reservoirs became the main supply of water for the town until two artesian deep wells were sunk near Cramptons Road in 1935/6. The Company sank two further bore holes as well as building water treatment works and reservoirs at the Cramptons Road site.

Water is pumped from the Cramptons site through an underground pipe to the Solefields reservoir. This pipe is to be supplemented by a second pipeline to be built in 2020/21 and Solefields reservoir is to be expanded to cater for the Town's growing population.

Part of the Cramptons site is now derelict and is scheduled for housing. The pumping station and treatment works operated by South East Water remain at the north of the site.

BREWERIES

Goldings Brewery

There were several large breweries in Sevenoaks who supplied the numerous public houses in the town.

Smiths Brewery in the High Street was built around 1830 by Robert Comfort who converted the stables of Suffolk House into a brewery. After he died, the business was sold and by 1865 was trading as James Smith and Company. At its peak, the brewery controlled 23 public houses in the area. Brewing ceased on the site in 1899 when the Company was sold to the Black Eagle of Westerham.

Holmesdale Brewery next to Bethlehem Farm in the High Street, was bought from Mr Allworth by John Bligh in 1862. Bligh built a larger brewery in 1882 to make the beer for Holmesdale Tavern and the many public houses he owned. Bligh sold the brewery and its tied houses to the London brewers, Watney Coombe Reid in 1911. By 1935 it had closed.

Goldings Brewery in Cramptons Road was built in 1901 and operated there until it moved to Wrotham Heath. The building later became a furniture repository for Youngs Department Store of Sevenoaks, before being demolished in 1970.

There were two corn mills at Greatness. Peter Nouaille, a Huguenot silk weaver, inherited one of the mills through his wife, and started a silk weaving business there in the 1760s.

Peter Nouaille invested heavily in the mill, using the fairly new technology of water powered silk spinning. The silk produced was crepe silk, silk with a crinkly surface. It was much used by Victorians for funerals. The business prospered and by 1766 about 100 people were employed there.

He built himself a substantial house, Greatness House, with formal gardens and a lake between it and the mill. He also built a row of ragstone cottages for some of his workers, which survived until the 1960s.

Peter died in 1809, and his son, also called Peter, took over the mill. By this time it was one of the largest industrial establishments in West Kent outside the Royal Dockyards. It was described as 140 feet long and 40 feet wide, and having at least two storeys.

In 1816 the son Peter was summoned to give evidence before a Royal Commission investigating the employment of children in mills. He admitted that he employed 80 children, some as young as six, for 12 hours a day with only an hour and half breaks. Children were employed because their small hands were better at getting the knots and tangles out of silk than adults. His excuse for employing such young children was that it kept them from running about the country and getting into all sorts of mischief!

The second mill remained a corn mill. This mill was destroyed by fire in 1928, but after rebuilding continued milling until 1935. It later became an upholstery workshop and has now been converted into apartments.

Greatness Corn Mill before conversion

Three of the cottages for the corn mill workers remain on the Seal Road. The 1881 Census records their occupations as millers and a red ware potter.

Corn Mill workers cottages in Seal Road

Remarkable Victorians

Elizabeth Purves

19th century Sevenoaks was fortunate to have found settling in it a succession of well-off, generous men and women who, for a variety of reasons, made their civic duty a serious concern. To a large extent their legacy shaped the pattern of our present day roads and houses and provided some important public buildings.

Fortunately Liberals and philanthropists with social and religious consciences like the Jacksons, the Thompsons, German, Kraftmeier, Swaffield and Swanzy used their influence and money to alleviate the social distress of their poorer fellow Sennockians. Perhaps their motives were mixed, yet their initiatives were generally beneficial to the community and did something to modify class distinctions and to improve social conditions.

Thomas Russell Crampton 1816 – 1888

Born in Broadstairs, Crampton was one of the great Victorian railway engineers and inventors. He designed and patented the Crampton Engine, with its large driving wheels in the rear of the firebox, long boiler, outside cylinders in the middle of the engine's length, and a low centre of gravity.

His many achievements included laying the first submarine telegraph cable between Dover and Calais in 1851, and building gasworks and waterworks in his home town of Broadstairs.

His work as a railway entrepreneur involved the construction of the Ottoman Railway in Turkey, and constructing lines in Kent for the London Chatham and Dover Railway (LCDR). He was appointed the contractor by the Sevenoaks Railway Company, formed in 1859, for building the railway line from Swanley to the Bat and Ball, passing through Eynsford, Shoreham and Otford. The line was completed in 1862. In 1861 he purchased St Johns Brickyard, on what is now the Vestry Estate, to supply the bricks needed for building the railway and for the Sevenoaks Tunnel which was started in 1863.

Crampton rented Greatness House from the Filmers who owned it at that time. When part of the Greatness Estate was sold in 1864, he bought 81 acres of land, forming the greater part of Greatness Farm and St John's Farm, which was developed into a small industrial area with brick fields, gas works, brewery, and working class housing. In 1868, he successfully bid to build a second gas holder at the Otford Road site.

By 1867 he was bankrupted, along with his partners, Edward Betts, and Sir Samuel Peto who was renting Chipstead Place, by their lump sum contract for building the Metropolitan Extension of the LCDR. Crampton managed to discharge his liabilities and by the time he died in 1888 he was once again a wealthy man.

Cramptons Road is named after him.

JAMES GERMAN 1820 - 1901

Major James German came from a textile family in Preston. Whilst living in Preston he was called to the Bar and twice stood unsuccessfully as a Liberal Member of Parliament. He moved to Sevenoaks in 1867 and rented Vine Court House from the Lambardes. When the Lambardes demolished Vine Court to make way for new housing, he bought 64 acres of land with William James Thompson of Kipppington, in the Bradbourne area for £18,500 to develop for housing. German retained a five acre plot for himself.

Thomas Graham Jackson living at Vine Cottage was a neighbour and fellow Liberal. Jackson designed a large house with a coach house and stables for him in 1874 on the plot in Bradbourne Road. The house, originally called Maywood, is now the Adult Education Centre.

German was a Justice of the Peace, at one time Deputy Lieutenant for Kent and held a Commission in the 3rd Royal Lancashire Militia from which he retired with the rank of Major.

A member of the Sevenoaks Local Board, he played a major part in improving sanitation for the town, and was instrumental in introducing the Darent Valley Main Sewage scheme.

He was also one of the leaders opposing Lord Sackville's attempt to restrict access to Knole Park, chairing the meeting in June 1884 which led to the townspeople marching to Knole and breaking down the obstructions put up by Sackville.

When he left Maywood, he moved to Belmont on the Vine where he died in 1901.

EMILY JACKSON 1840-1916

The Jackson family moved to Sevenoaks in 1867 and lived in Vine Cottage, Hollybush Lane. Whilst living there Emily's brother, Thomas Graham Jackson, met and married Alice Lambarde, daughter of William Lambarde of Sevenoaks.

Lambarde allowed Emily to use one of his cottages on the Vine in 1871 to nurse a young girl with tuberculosis. This was the start of the Hip Hospital. When the cottage was sold in 1876 with the rest of the Vine Court Estate, Emily's father first rented and then bought the house next door, number 2 Park Lane, for her to run as a children's hip hospital.

By 1897, there were 25 patients at 2 Park Lane which had expanded to include number 4 Park Lane, but still larger accommodation was needed to cope with the number of children with tubercular hips. A plot of land was purchased in Eardley Road and her brother, the architect Thomas Graham Jackson, designed a new hospital with 45 beds. The cost of £10,000 was funded by public subscription. The Sevenoaks Chronicle reported that when the foundation stone was laid, the great and the good of Sevenoaks assembled, including both Swaffield and Swanzy who had made sizeable donations. The ceremony was conducted by the Rev. H. P. Thompson. In 1902 she moved her patients and staff to the new building in a grand procession of prams and starched uniforms.

The old hip hospital is now a care home, called Emily Jackson House in memory of Emily.

Sir Thomas Graham Jackson 1835 - 1924

Thomas Graham Jackson, one of the most distinguished architects of his generation, and also a Royal Academician, moved to Sevenoaks in 1867 with his parents and his sister Emily. The family lived in Vine Cottage, Hollybush Lane. Whilst living in Vine Cottage, he met and married Alice Lambarde, daughter of William Lambarde of Sevenoaks.

Although his main works were for Oxford and Cambridge Universities, he designed some notable buildings in Sevenoaks, including the house Maywood (now the Adult Education Centre), in 1874, for his friend and fellow Liberal, James German.

Thomas and his father bought some land in 1878 in the centre of Sevenoaks, to build houses for working men and their families. The aim was to enable the poor to live in the town and not be pushed out to areas like Greatness which they regarded as unattractive with no room for gardens. Thomas designed the 24 cottages and a coffee house which later became the Lime Tree Temperance Hotel, as a small working class community. Called Lime Tree Walk, it is tucked away to the west of the London Road, and is Grade II Listed.

For his sister Emily, he designed the Emily Jackson Hip Hospital in 1901, a purpose built hospital of 45 beds off Eardley Road. He also planned St Nicholas' Church choir vestry in 1908-9, the chancel and organ chamber for St George's Church, Weald in 1872 and the Kippington War Memorial. The Building News of November 1896, records that he was the architect of the Cobden Road Board School built in 1877.

Jackson died in November 1924 and is buried in St Nicholas' churchyard.

EDWARD KRAFTMEIER (KAY) 1851-1916

Edward Kraftmeier who was born in Germany, was an explosives expert and a manufacturer of gunpowder. By the time he came to England in 1874 he was a wealthy man.

His business enterprises included owning a gunpowder factory, and being a director of the British South African Explosives Company, the Nobel Dynamite Trust Company, the Chilworth Explosives Company and the Central Exploration Company of Western Australia. He was also a member of the Ordnance Committee and a member of the Royal Institution.

Kratmeier gave up his German citizenship and became a naturalised British citizen in 1892, marrying Emmie Kay the same year. In 1907, he bought the country estate of Ashgrove, now the New School at West Heath, where he lived with Emmie until his death.

They had four children, but a son and daughter died at a young age. For his daughter Esme who died aged 12 in 1908, he commissioned a mausoleum to be built in Greatness Cemetery for her burial.

Kraftmeier was a generous benefactor to the town. In 1913, as a mark of his appreciation of his years in Britain and as a memorial to the late King Edward V11, he agreed to pay for the indoor swimming baths. Kraftmeier originally offered Sevenoaks Urban District Council £3,000, but when it was found that with various improvements they would cost double that amount, he agreed to pay the extra cost. The baths in Eardley Road opened in late December 1914. He stipulated that on two days of the week, the swimming bath should be reserved for certain hours for ladies and certain hours for gentlemen.

In 1915, due to the anti German feeling at the time, Kraftmeier changed his name by deed poll to Kay. He died suddenly aged 65 of heart failure at Ashgrove and is interred with his wife, young son and daughter Esme in the Kraftmeier Mausoleum.

HENRY SWAFFIELD 1834 –1912

Henry Swaffield was born in Cornwall but moved to Sevenoaks in 1876. He lived at Cornwall House, 20 Granville Road, having amassed a considerable fortune from the stock market.

He was a Justice of the Peace and a great benefactor to the town and the Wesleyan Methodist Church.

In 1894, the year he was elected to the Sevenoaks Urban District Council, he paid for a bandstand on the Vine and later for the band practice room in 1902. Brass bands were popular at the time as they were thought to provide a way to keep working men occupied and out of the pubs.

Swaffield leased the Market House from Lord Sackville in 1896, and after renovating it, gave the building to the YMCA for a reading room and social centre.

A strong Wesleyan Methodist, he was responsible for building and paying for most of the new Methodist Church in the Drive which opened in 1904. On land behind the church, he built the eight Retreat Almshouses and the Cornwall Hall. Swaffield also paid for the vacant plot next to the Church so that a library could be built. The building itself was a gift from Andrew Carnegie.

Swaffield died in 1912 and is buried in St Nicholas' churchyard. Swaffield Road on the Wickenden estate is named after him.

FRANCIS SWANZY 1854– 1920

The Swanzy family money came from their interests in trade in West Africa. Leaving the Gold Coast in the 1850s, Francis's father, Andrew Swanzy, built Quarry House, a large house in Kippington with 28 acres of land. Francis lived there with his parents, but later moved to Granville Road. After his father's death, Francis controlled the commercial interests of the family firm and used much of his wealth to benefit the town.

A philanthropist, Justice of the Peace and a Liberal, for many years he was a Member of the Sevenoaks Urban District Council, and twice elected as Chairman.

Swanzy had a particular interest in sanitation and the provision of housing for the working classes, investing in and supporting the Sevenoaks Artisans Dwelling Company when it was formed in 1903. He donated £7,000 to build Holyoake Terrace, cottages to rent for poorly paid clerks.

When the Urban District Council bought 12 acres of School Lands from Sevenoaks School in 1910, to provide the Hollybush Recreation Ground for the town, he donated £4,750, half the cost. As President of the Sevenoaks Bowling Club, he persuaded the Urban District Council to provide a bowling green for the Club at the new recreation ground.

In 1916, he was instrumental in establishing the Sevenoaks Day Nursery in Sandy Lane so that mothers could take employment whilst their children were properly looked after.

Swanzy was a governor of Sevenoaks School, and left £5,000 in his will to the School which enabled it to build new classrooms and science laboratories. The Swanzy Building is named after him.

LILIAN GILCHRIST THOMPSON 1859 - 1947

Mrs Lilian Gilchrist Thompson, wife of Henry Percy Thompson, vicar of St Mary's Church Kippington, was a remarkable lady.

Her brother, Sidney Gilchrist Thomas, discovered a method of de-phosphorising pig-iron which revolutionised the manufacture of steel. He also found that the slag which was formed when making steel could be used as a soil fertiliser. These inventions made him a large fortune. When he died at the age of 34, he entrusted to his sister the money arising from his patents to spend on doing 'good deeds'.

Lilian was a Liberal member of the Sevenoaks Urban District Council, involved in many good causes and a keen champion of women. She helped expose the evils of industrialism in shops, factories and dangerous trades. She was also involved in crusades for women factory inspectors and for trade boards in sweated industries.

When the Sevenoaks Co–operative Society wrote to her in 1898, she agreed to their request to donate two acres of land off St Botolph's Road for the erection of working class dwellings. In 1904 work began on building 25 houses in what is now St Botolph's Avenue for the Sevenoaks Tenants Association

She held strong views. As President of the Diocesan Societies for Befriending Women and Girls by Preventive and Rescue Work, she wrote a letter to the Spectator in 1928 about "the horrible results of permitting men who are, sexually, as dangerous beasts, to roam at will, attacking innocent victims – to be punished at the most by temporary imprisonment. I believe that men convicted of assaults on children be at once sterilised, and, if necessary, also segregated for life – having been proved unfit for life in a community".

Lilian had five children. Her three sons served in the First World War and each was decorated for gallantry. Her two daughters worked at the Cornwall Hall VAD Hospital.

Lilian died aged 88 at the Forge House, Otford.

WILLIAM JAMES THOMPSON 1817- 1904

William Thompson, who had made his fortune in the family firm of tea brokers, bought the Kippington Estate in 1864.

Although he owned Kippington House, he let it for much of the time and lived in other houses on the estate. In 1896 he lived in Kippington Grange, and after selling it in 1903, leased Kippington Court.

A man of deep religious convictions, Thompson was a church warden of St Nicholas' Church. His views were at odds with those of the rector, Thomas Curteis, so in 1878, he gained permission from the Archbishop of Canterbury to endow and build a new church, St Mary's, on his Kippington estate.

He was a Justice of the Peace, a Governor of Sevenoaks School and in 1888 High Sheriff for Kent. Thompson was also the chairman of Sevenoaks Water Company, one of the founders of the Cottage Hospital and donated the land for Drill Hall in Argyle Road in 1898.

Together with James German, he developed Bradbourne Park and Mount Harry Roads for large houses for the new rail commuters. He also set up Dunton Green Brickworks in 1862 which made fine quality bricks and tiles.

His fourth son was Henry Percy Thomson, vicar of St Mary's Church from 1895-1919.

He died in April 1904 and is buried in St Nicholas' churchyard.

Churches

Geraldine Tucker

In the 19th century, religion was still at the centre of community life with the Church of England remaining dominant. However, an official census taken in 1851 of attendance at all places of worship showed the increasing influence of the non-conformist churches. In Sevenoaks, new churches opened reflecting both the continued strength of the Church of England but also the burgeoning interest in non-conformity. Prompted by the restoration of the Roman Catholic hierarchy in 1850, there was also a Catholic revival in Sevenoaks towards the end of the century. All these changes were a response to the growing and increasingly diverse population of Sevenoaks.

St Nicholas Church was the sole Anglican church in Sevenoaks until the 1820s. New chapels of ease were then created for those who lived some distance from their parent parish church: St George's Sevenoaks Weald completed 1822; St Mary the Virgin Riverhead (1831); and St John the Baptist in St John's area (1858). All later became parishes themselves – Weald in 1861, Riverhead in 1864 and St John's in 1878. A separate parish was also formed for Kippington in 1877 with the new church St Mary's Kippington being consecrated in 1880. Non-conformist churches opened in the 19th century in Sevenoaks included St John's Congregational (1866); the Vine Baptist Church (1887); and the Wesleyan Chapel, Bank Street in 1853 replaced by a larger Methodist Church in The Drive 1904. Following the Catholic Emancipation Bill in 1829 and the restoration of the Catholic hierarchy in 1850, St Thomas RC temporary 'Iron Church' was built in 1880 and replaced with its present permanent building in 1896.

St John's United Reformed Church
St John's Hill

Prominently situated at the top of St John's Road/Hill, the foundation stone was laid in August 1865. The church opened a year later and was initially known as the "Congregational Chapel" and by 1896 as the "Congregational Church". With the amalgamation nationally in 1972 of most Congregational and Presbyterian churches, it is now called "St John's United Reform Church".

Designed by architect John Tarring in Gothic style of uncoursed ragstone from the quarries in Knole, its seating capacity of 500 initially proved over -ambitious especially as house building in the nearby area was slow and the expected congregation at first failed to materialise. When the cost spiralled rapidly to over £4,000, the building had to close for a short while due to financial difficulties. Additional costs were then incurred when the original 130 foot spire was deemed unsafe and had to be removed in 1880. It was replaced by pinnacles on its four corners which themselves had to be removed in the 1970s as they had also become unsafe. The church has however retained its tall tower to the south which now incorporates an attractive clock.

A church hall was built in 1881 in Hollybush Lane to accommodate the growing numbers in the Sunday school. Stone plaques reveal that the architect of this building was R H Hill, the builder W Wiltshire and the minister C Lankester BA with the stones themselves laid by A S Newton, Sheriff of London & Middlesex. Able to accommodate up to 350 people, the hall was used for many church activities and also for public meetings. During World War I, it became a VAD hospital for British and Belgian soldiers.

However, in 1991/2, St John's United Reform Church was remodelled with a floor inserted in the nave providing rooms below for meetings and associated activities and St John's Hall became redundant. It was sold and converted to private accommodation in the 1990s. Recently, there has also been some discussion about the Church's future itself; whether two United Reform Churches (the other is in Littlecourt Road) are needed in Sevenoaks.

St Mary's Church, Kippington

It was William Thompson who was responsible for the creation of the new Kippington parish. Initially a church warden at Sevenoaks parish church of St Nicholas, he found his evangelical views were at odds with the Rector, the Rev T S Curteis. Thompson successfully applied to the Archbishop of Canterbury to build his own church on his Kippington estate. The new parish was created in 1877. Some of the statutory marker stones laid at the time still exist. These show the extent of the new ecclesiastical parish boundary.

Pending the building of the new church, Thompson donated a plot of land in Granville Road and a temporary 'Iron Church' was erected. With their cast-iron frame and corrugated iron walls and roof, 'Iron Churches' were essentially pre-fabricated buildings that could be erected easily pending a long-term solution. The first place of worship in the new parish was therefore in this building which was dedicated in April 1878.

The foundation stone of the new St Mary's Church was laid in May 1878. The architect was John Marshall Hooker who built it of Kentish ragstone in Early English style. The consecration ceremony, at which the Archbishop of Canterbury, Archibald Campbell Tait, presided, took place in June 1880. One of the most expensive buildings in Sevenoaks at the time, the total cost of the new church was £12,500. Before her death in 1876, Thompson's sister, Esther, had already contributed £5,000. William Thompson provided much of the rest, including a further £2,500 set aside as an endowment. Methodist Henry Swaffield presented St Mary's with the Bible for the lectern, the Prayer Book for the reading desk and the Altar Services. With a seating capacity of around 450, St Mary's seems to have been well attended from the outset. Thompson's fourth son, Henry Percy, was the vicar from 1895 to 1919.

St Mary's Church is now statutorily listed with its fine decoration, both inside and out, still much admired. One notable feature is the World War I memorial outside the church. This was designed by Sir T G Jackson in 1919 and consists of an octagonal stone plinth surmounted by three octagonal stone steps decorated with laurel wreaths near the base and topped by a Celtic cross. The inscription reads *"In memory of the men of Kippington who died for their King and country in the Great War 1914-1918"*.

St Luke's Church, Eardley Road

As originally established, Kippington parish was bisected by the Sevenoaks Tubs Hill railway cutting. This made communication between the two parish halves difficult as St Mary's Church Kippington was on one side of the railway and the temporary 'Iron Church' building in Granville Road was on the other. William Thompson initially wanted to construct a pedestrian suspension bridge over the railway cutting but this was vetoed by the railway company. Thompson therefore proposed a new church building on the Granville side. Emily Jackson agreed to sell part of her Children's Hip Hospital plot to erect the new church, hence its name 'St Luke's' after St Luke the Physician.

While the initial design was by architect John Lee, St Luke's Church was built in stages. The first by Lee was completed in 1904 and the new church was consecrated in 1905. The second phase, by local architects Potter & Harvey, added a permanent nave in 1909. Accommodation for the sick children's carriages was incorporated in 1912/13. From the 1940s onwards, St Luke's was largely the responsibility of the curate at St Mary's for whom the parsonage was built in 1954/55. St Luke's continued as the daughter church of St Mary's until 1958 when it achieved partial autonomy as a 'Conventional District', leading to full independence as a separate parish in 1996. In 1998, the Millenium Project carried out further improvements to St Luke's Church, designed by Malcolm Green, which included a new parish room and bell.

VINE BAPTIST CHURCH, THE VINE

Opened in 1887, the Vine Baptist Church is a striking landmark feature situated at the junction of Park Lane. Salmon's 1891 Guide to Sevenoaks describes the new church: "*A new building in Kentish rag having 400 sittings and a spacious Sunday school adjoining.*" Designed by architect John Wills who also built the matching Sunday School in 1888, the church was built in Gothic style of coursed ragstone on land acquired in 1870 for the 'Particular' Baptists - a strict splinter group who split from the 'General' Baptists in Bessels Green in 1748. Around 1776, they moved into a small building on the London Road, now behind Graham Webb Hairdressers, thus becoming the first dissenting chapel in the town. There is a description of this small chapel in Jane Edwards' text (1792-1868) about her recollections of old Sevenoaks. A scrolled iron gate still exists today on the London Road marked 'Chapel House'.

Competition during the second part of the 19th century between the Baptist chapels and the new Congregational church on St John's Hill eventually resulted in most of the congregation of the 'General' Baptist chapel in Hartslands amalgamating with the Congregationalists when the new Congregational Church was opened on St John's Hill in 1866. Under the leadership of the well-known Baptist minister, teacher and local politician, John Jackson, the 'Particular' Baptists however resisted such amalgamation. Jackson also played a major role in the building of the Vine Baptist Church.

By 1899 the 'Particular' Baptist church still only had some 220 members although there were 140 children in the Sunday school. The church also had a strong interest in overseas missions. The latter in particular helped to ensure the church's survival. In 1924 the buildings were extended and updated, so creating the 'Spurgeon Memorial Hall' and a chapel keeper's cottage beside it. In 2000 the Spurgeon Hall was remodelled with a modern entrance to the side.

St Thomas of Canterbury RC Church
Granville Road

It was not until 30 years after the restoration of the Catholic hierarchy in 1850, that a temporary 'Iron Church' dedicated to the Holy Trinity was erected in 1880, helped by a generous loan from the Buchanan family who lived close to the new church. The 1881 census also records the Buchanan family's boarder, Father Ignatius Lazzari, who became the church's first rector.

It was Father Lazzari who secured a permanent building. By 1884, sufficient funds had been found to build a small chapel to replace the temporary iron building. The iron building was transferred to Chatham Hill Road at Bat & Ball, where it became for a time the headquarters of the St John Ambulance Brigade. The church architect Frederick Walters was brought in to design the new church which was built on the junction of Granville Road and Gordon Road. Opened in 1896 by the Archbishop of Westminster, Cardinal Vaughan, the new church, built in a simple Romanesque style with a spirelet, was dedicated to St Thomas of Canterbury.

The plan was always to extend the church once sufficient funds could be found. Donations came from an eclectic mix of donors, including the Duke of Norfolk, the 3rd Marquess of Bute, Empress Eugenie, widow of Emperor Napoleon III of France and Victoria Sackville-West. Walters was brought back to carry out the large extension which brought the building to its current length in 1926 and included the present saddle-backed topped tower. The Father Tom Quinn Memorial Porch is a recent sympathetic addition (1994) by Burns, Guthrie & Partners.

The Church's door to the front with Latin inscription and diagrammatic representation of the Holy Trinity on the front is a reminder of its original name. A key feature on the old 1884 building which is physically attached to the main church is the full-size statue depicting St Thomas of Canterbury on the upper outside.

METHODISM IN SEVENOAKS

John Wesley's first recorded visit to Sevenoaks was in October 1746 but the growth of Methodism in Sevenoaks essentially began in the 1750s when Amy George, a store keeper, offered hospitality both to Wesley and other visiting preachers who held meetings in her house in Hill's Yard, in the centre of the town. As the congregation grew, an upstairs room was first rented in the 'Granary' in Coffee House Yard in London Road and then a small chapel was built in Hill's Yard, opened by John Wesley himself in 1774. When that also became too small for its burgeoning congregation, a Wesleyan chapel, designed by W Pocock, was built in Bank Street, opening in 1853. A Sunday school was added in 1862. The Methodists stayed there for 50 years. The building, now commercial premises, is still recognisable as the old chapel and school.

Devout Methodist Henry Swaffield, made the move from Bank Street to The Drive possible. Swaffield bought the plot of land in The Drive and paid more than two thirds of the £7,000 cost of building the new Church. Designed by James Weir, it was built of Kent ragstone with Bath stone dressings. One of the defining landmarks of The Drive, it possesses a superb façade. Unusually for a Methodist Church, it has a prominent spire. Swaffield opened the Church in March 1904 with a silver key made especially for the occasion. The interior had state of the art facilities. It seated 600 and had a gallery, red granite pillars, a pipe organ and was even fitted with electric wires though electric light had not yet been installed in Sevenoaks. By the time of the Church's centenary in 2004, it was clear that some facilities needed improvement. A new pipe organ had already been installed in 2001 and in 2010, a new glass vestibule was added to the front of the building.

OTHER DENOMINATIONS

There were other religious groups of significance in Sevenoaks at this time, including the Quakers (the Religious Society of Friends). There have been Quakers in Sevenoaks since the 1650s. However, numbers declined in Sevenoaks from the 18th century such that Quaker meetings finally disappeared from the town in the 19th century. A revival took place when a Quaker meeting was re-established in Sevenoaks in the 1930s. From 1960, Quaker Meetings have been held in the Friends Meeting House at 30 Hollybush Lane. Built in 1870 and known as 'Knole Cottage', it had previously been a sanatorium for Walthamstow Hall School.

Another significant group in Sevenoaks is the Vine Evangelical Church. The Open Brethren were founded in the early 19th century and from the late 19th century have had their meeting place in Sevenoaks on the junction of Dartford Road and Hitchen Hatch Lane. Originally built around 1870 as a hotel, Vine Hall was never used as such. In the 19th century, it was notable for its local Sunday school as well as its mission work. A final group is the Christian Science Society which established itself in Sevenoaks in 1904 and now have a meeting place on St John's Hill.

Church schools, including Sunday schools, and overseas missions were very much a feature of life in Sevenoaks in the 19th century. The temperance movement and other social and leisure activities also tended to be church led. Today the overall picture is one of vastly declining church attendance and increased secularism. Although faith schools still remain in Sevenoaks, the future of some Sevenoaks churches looks uncertain.

Community & Civic Buildings

Geraldine Tucker

40 years after the arrival of the railways, the Town's population had doubled in size. It is easy to see why Sevenoaks, with its fresh country air and clean water supply, became a magnet for the well-off professional classes, who worked in London, but were keen to remove their families from an increasingly overpopulated, industrially polluted and disease-ridden city. The wealthy new arrivals with their demands for fine mansions, public buildings and other accoutrements drew workers of all kinds to the Town. They also brought their own ideals and initiatives which have left a lasting legacy.

An increasing number of community and civic buildings were constructed to meet the needs of an expanding and more sophisticated Sevenoaks community. As the Edwardian era approached, the old Sevenoaks, based on its small rural market economy, was disappearing. Its transformation to a large modern town was underway.

CARNEGIE LIBRARY

"It was from my own early experience that I decided there was no use to which money could be applied so productive… as the founding of a public library." This quote by the Scottish-American philanthropist Andrew Carnegie (1835-1919), self-made but one of the richest people in history, shows the emphasis Carnegie placed on this public facility, building over 2,500 libraries worldwide during his lifetime. Sevenoaks Urban District Council applied for a gift of £3,000 from Carnegie which he granted on condition that the Town provided the land, the books and all the running costs. It was Henry Swaffield who donated the land next to his new Wesleyan Methodist Church at the top of The Drive. The site had originally been known as the 'Long Pond'.

The Sevenoaks 'Free' Public Library & Local Museum, was opened with a gold key by Lord Avebury on 4th November 1905. Prior to this, only subscription libraries had existed in Sevenoaks. The building is a rare surviving Sevenoaks example of the architect Edwyn Evans Cronk, a prominent Sevenoaks figure. Built of red brick and stone with green slated roofs, the design has been described as *"eclectic, Jacobean in flavour"*. Inside the building, there is a plaque commemorating the generosity of both benefactors. Donations of books came from the public. A librarian was appointed in 1906. The library remained here until it became clear that larger premises were needed. The Kent County Library Service had taken over responsibility for the Sevenoaks library in 1974. A new purpose-built structure, funded by Kent County Council, was erected in Buckhurst Lane in 1986. Since then, the former 'Free' Carnegie Public Library has been used as offices.

THE RETREAT ALMSHOUSES

Keen to provide a 'retreat' for elderly people of limited means who might otherwise be forced to take refuge in the Workhouse, Henry Swaffield in 1904 built eight small cottages on land initially behind the newly erected Drive Methodist Church but now situated behind the former Carnegie library building. The memorial stone was laid on 6th April 1904 with the opening ceremony in November that year. Designed by the same architect as the Methodist Church - James Weir - the one storey cottages with attic were built of Kentish ragstone as a L-plan terrace in two groups; nos. 1 & 2 and then nos. 3 to 8 in a traditional collegiate style. The dwellings had porches with Tudor arched doorways and mullioned windows with slate roofs and prominent red brick chimney stacks. From the outset, the link with the Methodist Church was strong. Preference is still given to elderly people of the Methodist faith who have lived in Sevenoaks for at least ten years. The buildings were Grade II Listed in 1972. Much overdue renovation of the Almshouses took place in the early 1970s. They re-opened in September 1974. There are now only seven dwellings.

Swaffield not only gave the land and paid for the buildings to be erected but he also provided an endowment fund. A notable feature of the 'Retreat' as Swaffield named the place, is its fine cast-iron gates. Decorated in blue and gold under a semi-circular arch, they incorporate the 'Retreat' 1904 date inscription and Swaffield's initials 'HS'.

Having built the Drive Methodist Church and the Retreat Almshouses, Henry Swaffield wanted a Hall built to be used by the whole Sevenoaks community as well as church members. Designed by local architects Potter & Harvey and named after Swaffield's place of birth, Cornwall Hall opened in 1906. It stands behind the Methodist Church and consists of a large hall surrounded by a smaller hall and a

range of function rooms. It was constructed in local ragstone with Bath stone dressings. Lavishly equipped by Swaffield, it became a popular meeting place for activities of all kinds. The 1906/7 programme included talks on 'Temperance Reform' and 'Knole' - the latter by local artist and photographer Charles Essenhigh Corke - and a Foreign Missionaries meeting. The weekly chess club met here – the annual Congress of the Kent Chess Association was held in the Hall during Easter week in 1908, opened by the distinguished civil engineer Sir Douglas Fox, then living in Kippington Grange. The Hall was also probably the site of the first cinematograph show in Sevenoaks. The Sevenoaks Music Club's first concert was given in the Hall in April 1933 by the Stratton String Quartet. Over the years, Cornwall Hall has been used for numerous community gatherings such as concerts, charity fairs and fund raising.

Aside from its fine architecture, Cornwall Hall is also of historical significance. It was used as a hospital during World War I - commemorated by a plaque inside the entrance. Many large houses and halls in southern England became emergency hospitals and wards for men from the Western Front who were nursed by women of the Voluntary Aid Detachment (VAD). The Sevenoaks VAD nursed 3,000 wounded soldiers in the Cornwall Hall. Its commandant was Kathleen Mansfield, wife of Dr Mansfield. She was awarded the Royal Red Cross by King George V in March 1918. In World War II the Hall was used as a 'British Kitchen' restaurant.

EMILY JACKSON HOUSE

A striking example of Victorian private charity, this Grade II Listed building was originally known as "The Children's Hip Hospital". Emily Jackson was the founder and superintendent. Emily Jackson Close, where the building is situated, is named after her. Emily dedicated her life to helping children afflicted with tubercular hips, a common scourge in the 19th century. Initially renting a small cottage on the Vine, her father bought the property in Park Lane adjoining the family home and gave it to Emily to use as a small hip hospital. Between 1880 and 1892, the Jackson family added a new wing to accommodate the growing number of patients and a dispensary. When larger premises were required, Emily sought voluntary subscriptions for a new purpose-built hospital, raising over £10,000, and in 1901 was able to move to the two-acre site in Eardley Road. Her architect brother, Sir Thomas Jackson, designed the new hospital in William and Mary style to an unusual butterfly plan. Near the porch is a dedication stone laid by Viscountess Templetown dated 20th June 1901. The new Hip Hospital had beds for 45 children, a significant number at the time. The old building in Park Lane was sold and became the Mount Hermon Orphanage in 1905.

The new hospital sold part of its plot to enable St Luke's Church (named after St Luke the Physician) to be built in 1904 and has retained a close link with the Church. A special children's chapel was built in 1912. In the 20th century, new drugs to treat tuberculosis reduced the need for the children's hospital which ceased in 1958. It was then used for convalescent patients and later as a geriatric unit. Closing in 1988, it became derelict. In the late 1990s, the original building was sympathetically restored. It is now a private care home for the elderly.

THE OLD POLICE STATION & MAGISTRATES COURT

In the 19th century, Sevenoaks, like many small market towns, possessed a parish constable and a 'lock-up'. The wealthy estate land-owners also had their own private 'police' consisting of gamekeepers, stewards and bailiffs. Following the formation of the Kent County Constabulary in 1857, the traditional parish constable and antiquated lock-up were deemed no longer fit for purpose. Major changes were made to the old system of providing law and order in Sevenoaks. It was decided that the Town needed a 'First Class' Station to act as the headquarters of the Division with accommodation for a Superintendent, lock-up keeper and junior police constables and a Petty (Parish) Sessional courtroom.

A new purpose-built Police Station was built in the High Street near The Vine in 1864 at a cost of £3,000 opposite the old 'lock-up'. Along with a magistrates court, it also had enquiry and administrative offices and police cells. The new Station was built of yellow stock brick with red brick detail and a slate roof. Notable features were the stone 'Police Station' plaque under the eaves and the cupola or octagonal roof lantern on the top of the building. A ragstone wall with piers and cast-iron railings formed the boundary. The former Sevenoaks 'lockup' sited on the opposite side of the road became accommodation for the groom constable. By 1902, the old 'lock-up' was deemed unfit for human habitation, demolished, and two cottages built on the site initially for police accommodation.

Sevenoaks Police Station remained here until it was decommissioned in 1972 when a new station and court was built at Morewoods, London Road. The old building was converted to flats in the 1990s by Portland Homes but has retained its original features.

CONSTITUTIONAL CLUB

Now known as 'Sevenoaks House', and backing onto the Vine Gardens, this landmark building where Dartford Road and Seal Hollow Road meet the High Street, was originally the Constitutional Club. Built in 1889 by notable local architects, father and son Thomas and Percy Potter, it was intended for social and political meetings and contained billiards, smoking and committee rooms and a refreshment bar. Two gold sovereigns are said to have been buried in the foundations on the south side. A noticeable feature of this long, almost triangular red-brick building is its hexagonal turret which is surmounted by a timber lantern. The Club's adjoining Assembly Hall was on the north side of the building, on the site where the Vine Gardens' water feature is now situated. The Assembly Hall had seating for over 500 people and was a popular venue for dances, concerts and other public entertainments until it was destroyed by a bomb in 1940.

In its heyday, the Constitutional Club was one of the principal buildings in the Town. On 11th February 1950, Sir Winston Churchill delivered an election speech to the constituents of Sevenoaks about the Labour threat to the economy and the Empire from the first floor window of the Club. Despite its apparent popularity, the Constitutional Club was forced to close in 1957 due to declining membership. The building was sympathetically restored with many of its original features retained and turned into apartments in the late 1990s. The original 'Constitutional Club' inscription is still clearly visibly above the wide panelled door facing Dartford Road.

GREATNESS PARK CEMETERY
CHAPEL & KRAFTMEIER MAUSOLEUM

Greatness Park Cemetery is built on land that formed part of the Greatness estate. A six acre site was bought from the Filmer family by the Sevenoaks Urban District Council (SUDC) and opened as a public burial place in 1906 complete with a small Mortuary Chapel and Lodge. The SUDC passed it to Sevenoaks Town Council in 1974. The Cemetery – now some ten acres - was extended in 2003 to provide expected burial space for the next 45 years. The Cemetery contains sixteen War Graves, of which eleven are in two small special plots. The land slopes steeply towards the north and at its highest point visitors can admire spectacular views over the North Downs.

Mortuary Chapel

One of the Cemetery's notable monuments is the Grade II Listed Kraftmeier Mausoleum built of granite with carved friezes to front and side and a barrel-vaulted copper roof. The original architect is thought to be the distinguished Art Nouveau pioneer, Charles Ashbee. It was commissioned by the wealthy industrialist Edward Kraftmeier, owner of Ashgrove, as a memorial to his daughter Esme who died in 1908 aged 12 .

GREATNESS PARK CEMETERY
CHAPEL & KRAFTMEIER MAUSOLEUM

Part of frieze from side of
Kraftmeier Musoleum

Kraftmeier Musoleum

The two 4' high Portland stone obelisks with ball finials flanking the door were stolen in April 2007. They were never recovered; new ones were commissioned from Portland quarry, scaled from photographs of the originals. The work was paid for by a grant from the Ibstock Cory Environmental Trust (ICET). In 2011 after falling into disrepair, the mausoleum, which had been listed by English Heritage in 2003, was restored and the roof replaced with another ICET grant.

Part of mosaic ceiling of Kraftmeier Musoleum   The memorial plaque for Kraftmeier's daughter Esme

Inside the mausoleum is a highly decorative mosaic ceiling with gold banding and acanthus leaf design. As well as Kraftmeier's daughter Esme, his son, John Edward, who died aged 4 in 1901, is commemorated inside the mausoleum with a plaque. There is also a wall plaque in the vault in memory of the family's god-son Dawson Downing, who was killed while flying over Salisbury Plain in February 1915.

DRILL HALL

The Former Residence for the Sergeant Instructor

The Drill Hall

The possibility of war with France led to the formation of a Volunteer Rifle Corps in Sevenoaks in 1860 led by Multon Lambard of Beechmont. While there was a good response, Volunteers had to train in the large drying house of Bligh's brewery in the High Street with target practice taking place on the 'Volunteers Rifle Range' in Knole Park. The Volunteers headquarters was the 'Bricklayer's Arms' at 48 High Street. It was not until William Thompson gave a plot of land in Argyle Road in 1897 for the erection of a Drill Hall to mark Queen Victoria's Diamond Jubilee that the 1st Volunteer Battalion of the Royal West Kent Regiment, then billeted in Sevenoaks, gained its headquarters. The funds raised for this purpose included a residence for the Sergeant Instructor which was built physically attached to the Hall. The single storey Drill Hall and its adjoining two storey house, both made of striking red-brick, were opened in 1898. Among other things, it was fitted with an up-to-date gymnastic apparatus and Morris tubes for musketry practise.

In World War II the Local Defence Volunteers (Home Guard), formed in May 1940, and the 20th (Sevenoaks) Battalion of the Kent Home Guard both drilled here. The squadron of the Air Training Corps (ATC), which was formed in Sevenoaks in 1941, moved their headquarters to the Drill Hall in the 1960s. Today the Drill Hall is the home of the Kent Army Cadet Force Sevenoaks and also the ATC Detachment 2158 (Sevenoaks) Squadron. In addition to its military purpose, the Drill Hall has been used, among other things, by local amateur drama groups. The Drill Hall was a venue for musicals from the 1950s until the Stag Community Theatre was created in 1983.

Social Housing

Geraldine Tucker

The new rail links led to a doubling of Sevenoaks' population from 4,700 in 1861 to 9,700 by the end of the 19th century. Pressure for new housing became intense. Demand was particularly strong in the centre of the town and in the areas around the two new railway stations, especially Tubs Hill. Speculative property developers moved in to exploit these areas by building 'genteel' villas in newly laid out roads such as Granville Road, Gordon Road and Eardley Road, all named after notable people of the time.

The Town's expanding working-class population was hit hard. Needing to live near their place of work, they could not afford such housing. Many already lived in cramped, unhygienic conditions. In 1854, the Sevenoaks Oversee of the Poor, Joseph Bradley, referred to the noxious cesspool in the Shambles which he wrote was 7 ft long, 6 ft wide and 4 ft deep, *"..full of refuse and night soil, and the 'stench' from it is injurious to health, and that the walls and rooms of the adjoining cottages occupied by labourers and their families are discoloured by it to the height of 4 feet where they sit by their fireplace"*. A number of prominent Sevenoaks figures helped to rectify the serious shortage of affordable housing in Sevenoaks for those in need.

Together with his father Hugh, a retired solicitor, the distinguished architect Sir Thomas Graham Jackson bought a field in the centre of Sevenoaks. Jackson then designed and built 24 quality working-class dwellings with splendid views and communal gardens, ready for occupation in 1879. The principal aim was to build excellent affordable housing for the poor, close to their place of work. This ground-breaking

development was named Lime Tree Walk, a name it retains today. In his 'Recollections', Jackson wrote of his new buildings *"I had tried to make them beautiful within the proper limits of cottage building, not the cottage orne, which is detestable, but with that kind of simple grace which comes from plain sensible construction."*

FORMER LIME STREET TEMPERANCE HOTEL

Alcohol was cheap and drunkenness common, the effects of which were felt especially among the working-class. In 1882, Sir T G Jackson designed and built a 'Coffee House' in Lime Tree Walk, which later became the Lime Tree Temperance Hotel. Cycling became a popular activity in the late 19th century and by 1886, this building was also the headquarters of the local cycling Touring Club - hence its unusual 'cycle' weathervane. The hotel thrived initially but its popularity diminished in the 20th century. It was forced to close in the 1930s with the 'Sevenoaks News'

taking its place. Damaged by a bomb in October 1940, the building was largely restored after World War II. It became the Sevenoaks Business Centre in 1996.

St Botolph's Avenue & Holyoake Terrace

St Botolph's Avenue

Holyoake Terrace

The Sevenoaks Tenants Estate was set up in 1903 by the then thriving Sevenoaks Co-operative Society. Its foundation capital of £7,000 was donated by Frances Swanzy. The Co-operative Society's aim was to build good quality homes for junior city clerks, book-keepers and sales people to rent. These were the people who commuted to London by 2nd and 3rd class. The proposal was that the tenants should become shareholders and receive a dividend on their rent from the Society's surplus. The architect for both St Botolph's Avenue and nearby Holyoake Terrace was Raymond Unwin, the Garden City pioneer.

Two acres on the north side of St Botolph's Road, with unrestricted freehold, were donated by Lilian Gilchrist Thompson, wife of Rev H.P. Thompson of St Mary's Church, Kippington and sister to the famous philanthropist inventor Sidney Gilchrist Thomas. Work began in 1904 on the erection of 25 houses to form St Botolph's Avenue. Each had three bedrooms, kitchen, parlour, scullery and small back garden. 22 houses were initially built forming two rows facing each other. 17 of these were complete by 1906. The last three houses in St Botolph's Avenue were built in a terrace. All 25 houses were occupied by 1908.

A second site of about three acres was donated by Frances Swanzy, even closer to the railway station, which was named Holyoake Terrace after G J Holyoake, the pioneer of co-operative housing. A row of buildings was constructed with an adjacent recreation ground on land falling away from Oakhill Road. These 34 cottages were built in a mix of pairs and groups of four, some all brick, some part brick, with oriel or bay windows. Most were built and occupied by 1908 with the remainder by 1910.

ARTISANS DWELLINGS: CRAMPTON'S & MOOR ROADS

Plaque on Moor Road: 'Sevenoaks Artisans Dwellings Co Ltd. 1904'

Alfred J St George McAdam Laurie was another prominent Sevenoaks figure who sought to address the shortage of working-class housing in Sevenoaks. He formed the Sevenoaks Artisans Company in May 1903 whose 22 shareholders included Henry Swaffield and Francis Swanzy. Influenced by the Garden City movement, this body aimed to construct a "cottage estate" which as well as including dwellings for artisans, would also consist of shops and other essential buildings. By 1904, a terrace of 20 houses was completed and occupied in Crampton's Road followed by

another terrace of 19 dwellings in Moor Road, initially called Hales Road. A large plaque of the Company can still be seen on each terrace. Crampton's Road was named after Thomas Crampton, the eminent Victorian railway engineer. The Sevenoaks Artisans Company lasted until 1933 when it went into voluntary liquidation.

The terrace in Otford Road of six workers' cottages with terracotta plaque was built to commemorate Queen Victoria's Jubilee in 1897. Private companies also stepped in to help their workers. The Sevenoaks Gas Company built cottages for its workers in Otford Road. These were pulled down in the late 70s/early 80s – the land now occupied by the Wickes/Currys/Carpetright stores.

The Railway Company in 1903 built two rows of six workers' cottages, known as "Quarry Cottages", by the Halfway House.

SUDC: FIRST COUNCIL HOUSING

It was the Sevenoaks Urban District Council (SUDC), set up in 1894, who inherited the process of acquiring land and building good quality affordable housing for the working class in the 20th century. The land came largely from the break-up of the great estates. In 1913, the first Council houses were built in Greatness Lane, from former Greatness lands, followed in the 1920s by houses built in the Hillingdon area from the former Wildernesse estate. As the 20th century progressed, lands belonging to other former estates such as Bradbourne and Kippington, as well as the large mansions in the Solefields area, were bought and built on by the SUDC. The Right to Buy policy of 1980 led to many of these council houses going into private ownership. Sevenoaks District Council, the SUDC's successor, no longer own any housing. Their remaining council houses were transferred to West Kent Housing in 1989.

Schools

Geraldine Tucker

Education in England was largely linked to religious institutions until the 19th century with many schoolmasters expected or required to be in holy orders. However, schools funded by private philanthropy and "free" grammar schools, the latter open to children of any religious beliefs, became more common. At the beginning of the 19th century, Sevenoaks had two main schools; the Queen Elizabeth's Free Grammar School and the Anglican Lady Boswell's School – the former endowed by the will of William Sevenoke in 1432 and the latter by Margaret Boswell in 1692. In addition to some church provision, a number of small private schools also existed. A significant number of poorer children were left with no education. The Elementary Education Act of 1870 created compulsory education in England and Wales for primary aged children. This authorised locally elected School Boards to use public money to build and support new schools. The 'Sevenoaks' School Board formed in 1875 built a Board School in Cobden Road in 1877 and another in Bayham Road in 1895. As the Town expanded, more schools were built or formed, notably in the independent sector such as Walthamstow Hall, The New Beacon and in the 20th century, Sevenoaks Prep and The Granville School.

The education system was expanded and reorganised throughout the 20th century. The 1902 Education Act replaced the School Boards with Local Education Authorities. In Sevenoaks, Kent County Council took over the Boards' former role. Sevenoaks now has a wide variety of single sex and co-educational, independent and state schools, at both primary and secondary level. Many of the early private schools have disappeared or moved location. A number of the older school buildings survive today but the trend in the state sector has been towards new buildings or purpose-built schools. Bradbourne Girls and Wildernesse Boys schools merged in 2010 to form Knole Academy in Bradbourne Park Road. New schools have been built on the former Wildernesse site - co-educational Trinity School, opened in 2013, and Weald of Kent Girls Grammar Annex, opened in 2017.

WALTHAMSTOW HALL

"Few spots within 20 miles of London can compare with Sevenoaks in loveliness of scenery and reputation for health-giving properties."- The Christian World publication 1878. Walthamstow Hall is now a major girls' secondary school in Sevenoaks. It was, however, originally founded in 1838 in Walthamstow, then a village situated five miles from London, for the education of the daughters of Christian missionaries. By 1876, the railway had come to Walthamstow, the rural atmosphere had disappeared and the "village" had become a suburb of London. As Walthamstow, like much of Victorian London, became increasingly over-populated and unhealthy, the school was compelled to move. Sevenoaks seemed the ideal location.

The distinctive red brick purpose-built school building was designed by notable architect Edward C Robins. Opened in 1882, it was the largest and most expensive building in Sevenoaks at the time. Initially a boarding school, pupils other than those of the daughters of missionaries were admitted from 1886 and day pupils from 1904. In 1897, nearby Knole Cottage was purchased as a sanatorium since infectious diseases, even measles and mumps, could have serious consequences. Three acres of land adjoining the school were bought from Sevenoaks School in 1908 to provide a sports pitch and a garden. In 1921, the school agreed to offer a percentage of free places to girls from local elementary schools in return for an annual grant from the Kent Education Committee. A number of buildings have been added over the years although the main building has remained largely as original. The school received bomb damage in September 1940 which destroyed the old Gymnasium and the new Science Laboratory and Craft Room. Fortunately, all girls and staff remained safe.

WALTHAMSTOW HALL JUNIOR SCHOOL

As pupil numbers grew, Walthamstow Hall's Junior School moved to a nearby large detached Victorian house called 'Knole View' in Bayham Road which was purchased around 1938/9. The Junior School remained here until 1992 when Walthamstow Hall merged with private day girls' school St Hilary's and acquired the latter's site in Bradbourne Park Road. 'Knole View' then became the Sixth Form Centre.

Walthamstow Hall Junior School's new home in Bradbourne Park Road building was originally a splendid Edwardian mansion. It was built in 1903 – see front inscription - with stables and a lodge and initially called "The Limes", later "Goodberry" and then "Parkwood" by 1916. In 1944, it had become St Hilary's School. St Hilary's was absorbed within Walthamstow Hall after the two schools merged in 1992. Today, the building is known as Walthamstow Hall Junior School. Although there have been several later extensions to the building, the original façade with its distinctive corner turret is clearly discernible.

Main School Building

School Chapel

The New Beacon is a purpose-built preparatory school for boys. Designed by Edwyn Evans Cronk, the architect of the former Carnegie Public Library in The Drive, and built by local firm Durtnells, the school opened in January 1900. One of its first pupils was the World War I poet Siegfried Sassoon. The school originally catered for up to 60 full-time boarders. It now has around 400 day pupils with limited weekly/flexi boarding provision. The main school building is largely original but other buildings have been added, many since the 1980s. It was John Stewart Norman who founded The New Beacon School. In 1882, he took over the failing 'The Beacon School' in St John's Road. In five years, numbers were up to 58 boys, many from well-known Sevenoaks families such as Swanzy, Knocker and Curteis and the school was thriving again as a feeder for leading public schools including Eton, Marlborough and Tonbridge. By the mid-1890s, the school had outgrown the St John's site and Norman bought the 21 acres 'Clenches' field at Cross Keys from Lord Amherst of Montreal. With its extensive grounds, the New Beacon School was one of the most expensive of its kind in Sevenoaks at the time.

The School Chapel is a unique feature for a Sevenoaks preparatory school. Its construction in 1912 meant that boarders could avoid the long Sunday walk to Kippington Church. Dedicated by the Bishop of Rochester in 1912, the Chapel was re-dedicated in 2012. Inside, a Memorial tablet lists those who contributed to its building, many of whom were well-known Sevenoaks individuals. Two other Memorial plaques commemorate those former pupils who died during the two World Wars - 35 in World War I, including Charles Mills, heir to the Wildernesse estate, and Siegfried Sassoon's younger brother Hamo, and 75 in World War II.

THE GRANVILLE SCHOOL

A number of Sevenoaks schools such as The Granville School, a preparatory school for girls, are sited in converted Victorian mansions. The Granville School was founded with six pupils on VE Day in 1945 by Miss Ena Makin in no. 84 Granville Road. As it expanded, the school moved

Main School Building

to a larger house in Granville Road, Greystone Lodge, now demolished. In 1957, it moved to its current location in Bradbourne Park Road. Set in five acres of garden and woodland, the main building of The Granville School is a converted substantial 3-storey mansion built in the early 1880s and originally named 'Dornhurst'. It was built for Augustus Thorne, barrister at law, Middle Temple. He was typical of the type of wealthy middle-class commuter who moved to Sevenoaks at this time. Such people were keen for their families to grow up in the countryside, away from the increasingly polluted and disease-rife city of London.

Thorne had two sons who were both born in 'Dornhurst'. General Sir Andrew Thorne (1885-1970) served with distinction in both World Wars. In World War II, he played an important role in the defence of Dunkirk in 1940. After the German surrender in Norway in May 1945, he formally held the sovereignty of Norway until 7th June when King Haakon VII of Norway (who also had connections to Sevenoaks) returned from exile. Thorne's younger son, Captain Thomas (1888-1915) joined the Grenadier Guards and was killed at the Battle of Loos, France in 1915. Following her husband's death in 1901, his wife sold the house. 'Dornhurst' changed hands several times during the 20th century. It was divided into flats in the early 1950s before becoming The Granville School in 1957. Despite some alteration, the now locally listed main building is largely unchanged. It is commended in SDC's Character Area Assessment document for its scale, designs and materials and its reminder of the origins of the character area.

FORMER BOARD SCHOOLS:
FORMER COBDEN ROAD SCHOOL

The former Cobden Road School is an excellent example of a Victorian Board School. Following the 1870 Elementary Education Act, it was built in 1877. Thought to have been designed by E E Cronk, recent research has revealed that the architect was Sir Thomas Graham Jackson. Built of red brick and now locally listed, it has two tall buttressed gables with large Gothic style windows. A notable feature is the large stone plaque in the centre of the side chimney stack which bears the inscription 'School Board for Sevenoaks Public Elementary School for Infants 1877'. Initially an Infants school, it was extended in 1884 to include girls up to the age of fourteen. By 1899, the register showed an attendance of 193 girls and 131 infants – a total of 324 pupils. Built in a densely populated working-class area, there was no green space for play. During the 1960s, the children would walk to the grounds of Vine Lodge School in Hollybush Lane. In 1975, the school closed and it became the 'Cobden Centre', occupied, among others, by Age Concern. Most recently, it was granted planning permission for sympathetic conversion into residential accommodation.

St John's CE Primary School

Another former Board School building was constructed in 1895 in Bayham Road which became known as the Bayham Road Boys Elementary School. It is now St John's Primary School. St John's School existed much earlier than 1895. From the mid-19th century, the Church of England created a number of 'National Schools' with teaching centred on the Church liturgy. St John's National School for Boys and Girls was one of these. It was probably formed around the mid-1860s as it is clearly marked on the first Sevenoaks Ordnance Survey map of 1868, located in Quakers Hall Lane in a building opposite St John's Church. Numbers of pupils had increased by the time of the next OS map in 1896. St John's moved to its present site in Bayham Road in 1978. Its old school building was demolished and a block of flats built on its former land, now called 'Old School Court'. Notable features of St John's School current building include the inscription on the terracotta plaque on the front central gable - '1895 Sevenoaks School Board' - as well as the tile hung bell turret with decorated lead ogee roof.

Sevenoaks Prep School celebrates its centenary in 2019. Its beginnings were modest. In 1919, tradition has it that the wife of Sevenoaks School Headmaster, Mrs Garrod, began educating boys in the Cottage block who were too young to attend the main school. By 1921, the Rev C G Holland became Headmaster of what had now become a rapidly developing preparatory school. He

Former site of Sevenoaks prep School

bought no.4 Vine Court Road, later known as 'Old School House' and moved there with 35 boys. Mr M N Jukes took over the school in 1928. In ten years, pupil numbers had increased to 102. While the school continued to grow, it had limited space for expansion and no sports playing grounds of its own. In the late 1960s, the school acquired the tenancy of Fawke Cottage at Godden Green and an adjoining field and moved there where it remains today. It now has extensive grounds and pupil numbers of around 380. It became co-educational in 1991.

The Vine Court Road venue where the school existed for nearly 50 years is a tall detached Victorian villa which is locally listed. Built in the 1880s, it was one of the first houses to be completed in Vine Court Road. It became St Michael's Orphanage for Girls soon after it was built, run by sisters Ellenor and Isabella Johnson. By 1891 the orphanage, or the 'Little House' as it was then known, was already well established and had ten boarders aged between 2 years and 13 years. It was still functioning as an orphanage until 1920 although now under the auspices of the Church of England 'Society for Waifs and Strays'. During World War II, Sevenoaks Prep used the basement of the house as an air-raid shelter.

Street Furniture

Elizabeth Purves

Sevenoaks streetscape is greatly enriched by historic street furniture, which ranges from milestones to lamp posts, post boxes to cattle troughs, railings to drinking fountains. All can be seen in the town. Street furniture may be easily overlooked, but it provides us with fascinating insights into the ways that local authorities and charitable associations provided much needed services for the town.

Drinking Fountains and Troughs

The provision of free, fresh drinking water was one of the most pressing issues of the 19th century. Cholera and typhoid was rife, often due to polluted water.

The Metropolitan Drinking Fountain Association was founded in 1859. From its outset, the Association was closely related to the temperance movement because of fear the working man would drink cheap beer or gin rather than search out clean water. For this reason, drinking fountains were often sited close to popular pubs to offer an alternative to the 'evils of drink'.

Initially the Association aimed to improve the supply of drinking water, but within a few years had extended its work to cover horse and cattle troughs as well. The Association changed its name in 1867 to include Cattle Troughs. At the time, cattle were often driven long distances to market and horses ridden for miles without water. The troughs which remain in Sevenoaks are reminders of the presence of animals in the town.

Fountains

In the High Street, at the junction with London Road, the ornate drinking fountain was erected in 1882. Built of marble and iron work, it is inscribed *"The gift of an inhabitant of Sevenoaks"*. It no longer functions as a fountain, but is used as a base for the signpost.

High Street Fountain

TROUGHS

The Association placed several granite troughs in the town. These troughs are no longer required for their original purpose and are maintained by Sevenoaks Town Council as planters.

Cattle trough in the High Street

The cattle trough in the High Street at the junction with Seal Hollow Road was erected in 1882, donated by Mr Hooper. It bears the inscription *"The gift of an inhabitant of Sevenoaks"*, on one side, and *"Metropolitan Drinking Fountain and Cattle Trough Association"* on another. At the southern end of the trough, there is a spout for drinking water. The cup which was attached by a chain no longer survives. The trough was originally outside the old Police Station but was moved to its present spot by request of the Local Board in May 1893.

Cattle trough at St John's Hill

Further north at St John's Hill and Bradbourne Road junction, there is another cattle trough with a spout for drinking water, inscribed with the words *"Erected by public subscription March 1886"*. The amount raised by the subscription is recorded by the Association as £77.

Trough in St Botolph's Road

In St Botolph's Road, near the junction with the London Road, another trough can be found. Made of polished pink marble the inscription reads *"Presented to the Town of Sevenoaks 1904 by Alfred St George MacAdam Laurie, Chairman of Sevenoaks Urban District Council"*.

Most of England's milestones were erected in the 18th century. Turnpike trusts were set up by Acts of Parliament to create new roads, as well as maintaining existing ones. They charged tolls and from 1766 were required to mark every mile with a stone. These milestones would inform travellers of direction and distances. They are typically located at the side of the road.

Three milestones have been identified in Sevenoaks. One on the Tonbridge Road, an original ragstone mile post for the toll road, one on the Seal Road with a later plate reading *"Maidstone 15 Godstone 13½"* and one on the north side of Bradbourne Vale Road close to the entrance to Knole Academy. The replacement plaque reads *"Maidstone 16 miles Godstone 12 ½ miles"*.

Milestone. Tonbridge Road

Milestone. Seal Road

Milestone. Bradbourne Vale Road

Boundary markers identify the edge of a land boundary; they mark a border.

There are two boundary markers in St Botolph's Road, thought to have been placed there in 1871, to mark the boundaries of St Botolph's Estate. One is at the Vine end of St Botolph's Road, and the other at the junction with Pound Lane.

St Botolph's Road and Pound Lane

St Botolph's Road

In South Park against the wall of the Coach House at the beginning of the footpath to Kippington, a marker stone dated 1877 shows the boundary of Kippington parish.

South Park

A further Kippington boundary marker is in Brittains Lane, on a path from Brittains Lane to Kippington via Redlands Road.

Brittain's Lane

Another Kippington parish marker is outside 24 Oakhill Road.

Oakhill Road

Letter boxes were first introduced in Jersey in 1852 on the recommendation of a Post Office Surveyor, the novelist Anthony Trollope. The public liked them. Provided you had bought postage stamps in advance, you no longer had to walk to a Post Office to post your letters. At first the boxes were painted green, but after 1875, they were painted red. Post boxes still have the initials of the reigning monarch marked on them.

VICTORIAN LETTER BOXES

A number of Victorian letter boxes remain in Sevenoaks. The Victorian wall box at the old Tuck Shop in the High Street opposite Sevenoaks School, is a rare Ludlow type box. Ludlow boxes with their distinctive enamel plates bearing the royal cipher and the words POST OFFICE LETTER BOX were made for use at sub post offices. The enamel plate of this one has been changed from the original Victorian, but otherwise it is still as it was when placed there in 1898.

Ludlow box at the old Tuck Shop

Other Victorian post boxes can be found outside 33 St Botolph's Road, on the corner of Holmesdale Road, outside 38 Granville Road, between 2 and 4 Burntwood Road, and on a pillar at 48 London Road. The Victorian box attached to the wall of St Mary's Gate House in Oakhill Road is Grade II Listed.

Victorian letterbox at St Mary's Gate House

Edwardian letterbox in Blackhall Lane

EDWARDIAN LETTER BOXES

An Edward VII cast iron letterbox is strapped to a post in Blackhall Lane at the junction of the Lane and footpath to Knole Golf Course. This is the only remaining Edwardian letter box in Sevenoaks.

GEORGE V LETTER BOXES

A number of George V letter boxes remain in the town with the letters G R in capitals embossed on the front. A wall mounted, Ludlow pattern box is in the London Road near the junction with Argyle Road. George V boxes can be found in St Botolph's Road, Seal Hollow Road, Woodland Rise, Solefields Road, Bradbourne Vale Road and Linden Chase

George V box in Seal Hollow Road

GEORGE VI LETTER BOXES

There are still a few George VI letter boxes in the town. The George V1 boxes have the letters G R in script with a small "vi" between the two letters. A wall mounted box is in South Park. Boxes set in brick pillars with concrete roofs are in the Rise at the corner with Garth Road, in Bosville Road and in Grove Road.

Wall mounted George VI box in South Park

ELIZABETH II LETTER BOXES

Hardly surprisingly, there are a large number of these, including many of which are cylindrical. The cylindrical boxes were first designed in 1857, but by 1887, improvements had been made and the new design included the reigning monarch's cipher. Six cylindrical boxes are to be found marching down the High Street like soldiers. The ones outside Lloyds Bank, the former Tescos and the Hollybush Parade are marked George V, and the other three, outside Knocker and Foskett, the old Constitutional Club and St John's Hill, are from the current Queen's reign and marked E II R.

Elizabeth II pillar box outside the old Constitutional Club

The High Street was first illuminated by gas lanterns on metal standards in 1840. The gas came from the gas works established in 1838 in Hartslands. The Sevenoaks Advertiser of June 1840 recorded *"the street was filled with a brilliant illumination and gas gave forth its pure clear light, increasing the comforts and to the convenience of securing the property of the inhabitants"*. A month later, a letter in the Advertiser gave a contrary view, saying that *"the gas lamps emitted an odious stench, there was a constant hiss of burning, and the lamp light was small and dim"*. Although the light provided was meagre compared to today's street lights, they provided some light when it was dark and made the town safer at night.

Until street lamps could be automatically lit and extinguished, lamplighters would work their way round the streets at dusk and dawn. Armed with long poles, they would light or extinguish each lamp in turn. Some lamp standards still have a T bracket for the lamp lighter to rest his ladder. 35 Grade II Listed gas lamps remain in Sevenoaks, many of which, dating from 1890, are in Kippington.

In 1975, the Sevenoaks Chronicle reported that 265 of the old gas lamps in the town were to be converted to North Sea Gas. These lamps were later converted to the much cheaper electricity.

Lamp opposite St Mary's Church

Lamp showing the T bracket

BENCHES

Throughout the town, there are benches in open spaces. Benches are needed to let people sit down, whether it is to watch the cricket on the Vine, enjoy a view or just have a rest.

Memorial Bench on Vine Waste

In 2018 Sevenoaks Town Council installed two metal benches as part of their programme to commemorate World War I. The first bench was installed at the Vine Waste opposite the War Memorial and the second is in the Upper High Street Gardens. In celebration of the 100 years anniversary of the Armistice, the town was decorated with thousands of knitted poppies provided by volunteers. The Town Council have also installed two wooden benches in Vine Gardens in honour of the marriages of Prince William and Kate Middleton in 2011, and Prince Harry and Meghan Markle in 2018.

RAILWAY TUNNEL VENTS

Tunnel vent in Oak Lane

Work on the Sevenoaks railway tunnel began in 1863. The tunnel which ran under the Greensand Ridge from Tubs Hill to near the Sevenoaks Weald, was almost two miles long. Access shafts had to be built for the navvies to work in the tunnel, and also to allow for ventilation. 13 vents for the tunnel were constructed. There is a fine example in Oak Lane. The shaft, number 13, at the northern end of the tunnel, was lined with bricks and topped with a brick turret.

SEWER VENT PIPES

Sewer vent pipes, also known as a stink pipes or stench poles, often 20 to 30 feet high and hollow, are made from cast iron and painted various colours. They may have fluted columns around the bottom and studded rings. Their purpose was to vent gas from the sewers under ground, releasing it high above street level so that the stench would not offend passersby.

St Mary's Kippington, St Botolph's Road, Vine Court Road, Linden Chase

TELEPHONE BOXES

K6 Listed telephone box in the High

Originally public telephones were put into shops, post offices and railway stations, but by 1900 a variety of kiosks had begun to appear on the streets as well. The first national standard design was the Kiosk Number 6, which was red with a domed roof, designed by Sir Giles Gilbert Scott and introduced countrywide in 1936.

A few of these K6 red telephone boxes remain in Sevenoaks. There is a Grade II Listed box outside the HSBC Bank in the High Street. Another, which was in Blackhall Lane, has been moved to the Vine. Now maintained by the Town Council, this box on the Vine has had a defibrillator installed inside, a good use of a redundant box.

ROAD SIGNS

In contrast to the current proliferation of signs, before the advent of the motor car there were few traffic signs. Old cast iron signs show the directions at two key junctions in the town.

Fingerpost at junction of High Street and Seal Hollow Road

The sign attached to the former water fountain in the High Street, points the way south on the A21 to Hastings, north on the A21 to London, and north east on the A225 to Dartford.

Metal signs are attached to the Victorian gas lamp at the junction of the High Street with Seal Hollow Road, showing the routes to Maidstone, Dartford and Hastings.

RAILINGS

Bollards and railings were set up to prevent encroachment of vehicles on to the pavement. There are some fine Victorian iron railings painted white on both sides of the Upper High Street.

PUMPS

Before water was piped to houses, people had to rely on springs, ponds, wells and pumps. Some of these Victorian pumps survive. A cast iron pump with handle can be found outside no.16 Six Bells Lane.

Pump in Six Bells Lane

Recreation and Leisure

Elizabeth Purves

During the second half of the 19th century when working hours began to be regulated by legislation, there was a great upsurge in leisure pursuits. Parks, gardens, and libraries were provided and paid for by Victorian philanthropists as well as the Local Board. The first cinema, the Elite Palace in Tubs Hill, opened in 1912, followed by the swimming baths in Eardley Road in 1914. Cycling became popular with the Lime Tree Hotel a meeting point for cyclists, and the new railway offered the opportunity for day trips to the seaside.

VINE PLEASURE GARDENS

The first public park in Sevenoaks was the Vine Pleasure Gardens, bought by the Local Board for £2,000 in 1890 from Lionel Sackville. The deeds held by the Town Council indicate that it comprised of three rods and eight and a half perches, and adjoined the premises of the Sevenoaks Constitutional Club.

Public gardens provided a place for people to meet, listen to music and walk in pleasant surroundings. The Gardens, now owned by the Town Council, include flower beds, a pergola and a fish pond with a wooden bridge. The Sevenoaks Guide of 1901 describes them as *"tastefully laid out with flower beds, asphalted paths and rustic shelters"*, and notes that children were allowed to play on the grass area.

VINE BANDSTAND AND PRACTICE ROOM

A bandstand became a staple feature of public parks, providing concerts for people to enjoy. A band was formed in Sevenoaks in 1890 and a bandstand placed in the Vine Pleasure Gardens with money donated by Henry Swaffield. The old Cricketing House was demolished and the Bandstand replaced it. A plaque erected by the Town Council describes the Bandstand, manufactured in Glasgow in 1894, as an open sided octagonal building, constructed of random rubble at low level, supporting a tarmacadam base with cast iron ornamental columns and balustrading covered by a slate roof. Its acoustics are excellent. Although the Town Band no longer exists, regular concerts are provided during the summer by the Town Council. The Bandstand was renovated in 2014 with a grant from the Cory Environmental Trust.

The Band Practice Room, adjacent to the Bandstand, was erected in 1902 and again paid for by Henry Swaffield. No longer required as a practice room, it was converted in 2015 to a community café, run by the Town Council.

The Vine is one of the oldest cricket grounds in existence. Games were mainly played between different parishes or land owner's teams. There were often with high stakes on the outcome of the games, teams being made up of owners and estate workers. Master and servant having the same interest was a unique occurrence.

The first recorded game on the Vine is believed to have been in 1734. The bowling was underarm, the bat shaped like a hockey stick and the wicket consisted of only two stumps and a bail. The Vine Club owns a cricket bat made by William Pett of Sevenoaks in 1745. It is made of willow and has a curving round end. Pett (1710-86) was the earliest recorded cricket bat maker in Kent.

The Club also owns a silver snuff box from 1818 which was passed around after Club dinners. Anyone dropping it was fined two shillings and six pence or a bottle of wine.

The Vine Ground was given to the town in 1773 by the 3rd Duke of Dorset, John Frederick Sackville of Knole and a keen cricketer. The Town Council now own the land and the Club has to pay them two peppercorns annually. In return, the Council has to give Lord Sackville a cricket ball if requested, every year.

A Bicentenary Cricket Match was held in July 1934, to mark the anniversary of 200 years of cricket on the Vine. The players were dressed in costume of the period when the first match was played on the 23rd August 1734 between the Gentlemen of Sevenoaks and the Gentlemen of Sussex.

In 1850 the Pavilion was built for the Countess of Amherst who let it to the Cricket Club. It replaced the old Cricketing House. When the Local Board bought the Vine land in 1890, the pavilion was included in the purchase price. During the First World War, the YMCA used the Pavilion as a canteen for troops who had taken over the ground as military parade ground. When the Army moved out at the cessation of hostilities, hardly surprisingly, the ground was in an appalling condition and needed much work to get it fit for play again..

The Pavilion fell into disrepair and was reconstructed and officially opened by Lord Sackville in 1937. The white weather boarded building, was extended and refurbished in 1957 and again in 1975 and is now Grade II Listed.

The Pavilion is the home of both the Cricket and Sevenoaks Hockey Clubs. The Hockey Club merged with the Cricket Club in 1973, to form the Sevenoaks Vine Club. The Hockey Club play on the Hollybush All Weather pitch, and use the pavilion in the winter season, the Cricket Club in the summer.

TEA HUT

The former summer house in the garden at Solefield House was moved to the northwest corner of the Vine in 1951 for use as a tea hut for spectators. The thatched roof was burnt down by arsonists in 2006 and repaired by the Town Council. The Tea Hut is now used for storage.

VINE WASTE

The Vine Waste comprises of two acres of land to the north of the Cricket Ground. It was given by Lord Sackville to the Urban District Council in 1921. The deed of transfer held by the Town Council who now own the land, states the following conditions. It is to be used and maintained as a site for a public memorial to those men of Sevenoaks who fell in defence of their Country in the Great War, and for an open space and place of public recreation. The grant of land requires payment of seven acorns each year. Local residents successfully fought off a planning application to turn it into a temporary car park in 2018.

THE GREAT STORM AND THE SEVEN OAKS

After the Great Storm

Seven oak trees representing the name of the town were planted at the North end of the cricket ground in 1902 to commemorate the coronation of Edward VII. Six of these trees were uprooted by the 1987 Great Storm, often referred to as the hurricane, but replacements have since been planted. A time capsule containing documentation of the disaster has been buried in the ground.

The only 1902 Oak left after the Great Storm

Upper High Street Gardens

Upper High Street Gardens. Upper garden

Upper High Street Gardens. Lower garden

At the south end of the town, are the Upper High Street Gardens. These were given to the town in 1949, by Miss Joan Constant, who lived in the Old House on the other side of the High Street. The gardens, adjacent to Six Bells Lane, were given as a tribute to Miss Constant's parents. There is a memorial tablet to them set in the northern boundary wall. The small garden of 0.25 acres, enclosed by brick walls, is now owned by the Town Council. It provides a quiet haven from the traffic in the Upper High Street. In 1995 there was a rose planting ceremony for the 50th anniversary of the United Nations. Four flowering cherry trees were planted by the local Women's Institute in 1999, and fifteen rose trees in 2009 by the Girl Guides to celebrate their centenary. One of the two World War I memorial benches commissioned by the Town Council was placed in the gardens in 2018.

KIPPINGTON MEADOW

Since 2005, the Town Council have owned and maintained Kippington Meadow. It was given to Sevenoaks Urban District Council in 1913 by the Rev. Percy Thompson, son of W.J. Thompson of Kippington, on the promise "that the natural beauties of the land should not be interfered with". The three acre park was originally part of the Kippington estate. In 2018 the Town Council obtained grant funding to install a play area in the Meadow. Within the Meadow there is also a water fountain built from lumps of ragstone and concrete. The inscription records that it was donated by the Rev. Percy Thompson.

Other recreation grounds now owned by the Town Council include Greatness Recreation Ground, Knole Paddock and Raley's Field.

The land for the Greatness Recreation Ground was originally acquired by Sevenoaks Urban District Council from the Filmer estate in 1918. Since 2007 it has been owned by the Town Council who have installed a 3G sports pitch, a skateboard park, an outdoor gym and new playground equipment. The thriving Sevenoaks Football Club is based at Greatness.

Knole Paddock, originally owned by Knole, was bought by Sevenoaks Urban District Council in 1929. The 11.7 acre site is used for rugby and cricket. The adjoining 9 acre Raley's Field, bought by the Kent County Council at the same time is used for football and tennis. Both sports fields are now owned by the Town Council. Sevenoaks Rugby Club and the Clarendon Tennis Club are based there.

HOLLYBUSH RECREATION GROUND

In 1510, 15 acres of the old Hillborough estate were given to Sevenoaks School by a group of local townsmen, including William Pett and Richard Blackboy. Known as the School Lands, they were let as farm land by the School, and later used as for cricket. In 1910 the School sold 12 acres to Sevenoaks Urban District Council to

provide a recreation ground for the town. Half the cost of the £4,750 purchase price was donated by Francis Swanzy, who as well as being a School Governor, was also Chairman of the Council. The remaining three acres were bought by Walthamstow Hall School. Now owned by Sevenoaks District Council, the recreation ground includes an all weather hockey pitch leased by the Hockey Club, tennis courts, an indoor and outdoor bowls rink, a flat grass area for informal recreation, a play ground and a café in the lodge.

BRADBOURNE LAKES

The park was originally laid out between 1740-1761 by Henry Bosville, as a picturesque landscape of lakes and waterfalls, forming the setting for Bradbourne House. When the house was demolished and the land sold for development in 1927, Sevenoaks Urban District Council bought the chain of lakes and the seven acre park for use as a public park in 1935.

Six interconnecting lakes were made by damming a branch of the River Darent which flows northwards through the Park. Two of these were later joined making the present total of five. The park is an hour glass shape, roughly divided in half by Betenson Road. The ground gently slopes from south to north, allowing shallow waterfalls to carry water from one lake to the next when there is sufficient maintenance. Over the years the lakes have become silted and are in urgent need of repair.

The Influence of Arts & Crafts on early 20th Century Buildings

Geraldine Tucker

The Arts & Crafts Movement began in the UK in the late 19th century and quickly spread to Europe and North America. It lasted until it was eventually displaced by Modernism in the mid-20th century. In essence, it was a reaction to the mechanism of the Victorian industrial age with its huge factories and mass-produced goods. It revived simple traditional craftmanship, utilised local materials, and often used medieval, romantic and folk styles of decoration. The writings and work of national figures, such as William Morris and John Ruskin, inspired architects local to Sevenoaks. C R Ashbee, who in later life lived in Seal, was one of these. However, it was English architect Mackay Hugh Baillie Scott (1865-1945) who is most associated with this movement in Sevenoaks. Baillie Scott's work is particularly evident on the Wildernesse estate. Other architects who followed the Arts & Crafts trend in Sevenoaks include Charles W Bowles, J Leonard Williams and local architect Charles J Cable.

Not all of Baillie Scott's contemporaries who worked in Sevenoaks followed the Arts & Crafts movement. Dame Jane Drew, whose early work can be seen on the Wildernesse estate, later became involved in the Modern Movement. However, in the early 20th century, the influence of Arts & Crafts extended widely across the whole artistic field. The renowned sculptor, Arthur G Walker, exhibited multiple works at the Arts & Crafts Exhibition Society in 1916 - the Grade II Listed 1920 War Memorial on The Vine, right, is a striking example of his work.

WILDERNESSE ESTATE

In Pevsner's Architectural Guide 'Kent: West and the Weald', John Newman writes of the Wildernesse Estate *"By 1939 about fifty houses had been erected, thirteen by Baillie Scott & Beresford. So this is an excellent place to study their late Arts and Crafts approach, evoking home by deep sheltering roofs that sweep down low and big reassuring chimneystacks, and their handling of materials, white plaster, brown brick and red tile hanging, but few exposed timbers. Siting and planting, which half hide, half reveal, also play their part."*

In 1924, Percy Harvey bought a large portion of the original Wildernesse estate and proceeded to develop it. The plan was to erect fine buildings but also preserve the characteristics of the countryside. New roads Parkfield and Woodland Rise therefore had the appearance and character of country lanes with grass verges flanked by substantial hedges. For the design of the Wildernesse properties, Harvey sought the services of many of the major contemporary architects, especially those of the Arts and Crafts movement. The houses designed by M H Baillie Scott and his partner A E Beresford are judged the best works of this era and building type and include a number of Grade II Listed buildings. Baillie Scott's early involvement with the first houses on the Wildernesse Estate is also thought to have contributed towards attracting other Arts & Crafts architects to the area, a number of whom practised close to his Grays Inn studio. These include C Cowles Voysey, L R Parratt and Edgar Ranger as well as notable local architect Charles Cable. Dame Jane Drew's early work can also be seen here in High Weald, Parkfield. At a time when architecture was a male-dominated profession, she went on to become arguably the most distinguished British female architect of the 20th century.

Kilnwood, Blackhall Lane by Baillie Scott

Built around 1927, the locally listed Kilnwood contains an abundance of Arts & Crafts features in the traditional country Manor House style. It is a complex design, with characteristic deep tiled roofs and dormers.

Godden House, Blackhall Lane by Baillie Scott

Less elaborate than Kilnwood but built at a similar time around 1927, locally listed Godden House nestles in a slight dip in the ground and thus appears to grow organically out of its plot. It possesses Baillie Scott's typical complicated roofline and tall corbelled chimneys.

Little Croft, Woodland Rise by Baillie Scott

Built around 1928, locally listed Little Croft is an excellent example of Baillie Scott's Arts & Crafts work with white rendered walls and original red clay tile roof and some black painted timber external decoration.

Baillie Scott's Dentistry, Dartford Road

Purpose-built early 20th century dentistries were rare. Baillie Scott is known to have designed only one, in 1927/8 in Dartford Road, for Dr E Wilfred Fish. Dental surgeon Dr Fish was a leading dental researcher who was knighted in 1954 for his work. More famously, he was Sir Winston Churchill's dentist. Churchill suffered from dental problems throughout his life and Fish was instrumental in designing and fitting the gold-plated dentures that were so important for Churchill's public speaking. The dentistry was bought in the late 1930s by fellow dentist Robert Eustace and the practice continues today as 'Eustace & Partners'.

Baillie Scott designed the now Grade II Listed one-storey building in neo-Georgian style, rendered with red brick dressing, a hipped tiled roof and two side tall red brick chimneystacks. Notable features include the central atrium with its octagonal glazed dome.

THE DRIVE COTTAGE, THE DRIVE

The architect Charles William Bowles began his training in 1884 and commenced practice in London in 1897. He designed a number of houses in Sevenoaks in the early part of the 20th century. His initial work – an Edwardian pair of mirror-image semi-detached properties in Arts & Crafts style - was near the newly erected 1904 Methodist Church at the top of The Drive. Having completed this by 1905, he went on to design 'The Drive Cottage' in 1909 for local artist Mary Heathcote Batchelor (see above). Bowles' later works in Sevenoaks include the imposing Grade II Listed St Mary's Gatehouse built in 1915 in Tudor style with attached steps, seat and drinking fountain. It was commissioned by the Rev Henry Percy Thompson of Kippington Church as a memorial to his parents. Another Grade II Listed property Bowles designed is 'Northdown', in Grassy Lane in Arts & Crafts style in 1924.

Bowles designed the Grade II Listed 'The Drive Cottage' in an Arts & Crafts Kentish Vernacular style which (externally at least) has the appearance of a traditional Wealden hall house. The steeply pitched roof contains an artist's studio in the attic space hence its triple hipped dormer with nine leaded light casements providing north light. The gables are tile hung and imposing brick chimneys stand at each gable end of the house.

FORMER KNOLE VIEW ESTATE, BAYHAM ROAD

Arts & Crafts architect J Leonard Williams drew his inspiration from his studies in Western Europe. Leonard Williams came from Harpenden in Hertfordshire and had worked for architect J B Wade for 15 years before setting up practice on his own in 1897. Around 1900, he was commissioned by the Hilder Daw family for what was termed the 'Knole View Estate' development.

Williams designed a trio of properties in Bayham Road, described by architectural historian John Newman as *"an extraordinary display of stylistic diversity".* These three pairs of large semi-detached houses were built on the same 'H' plan with each pair exhibiting different interpretations of the Arts and Crafts style.

All three properties are now Grade II Listed.

Dutch style Bayham Road

The first two-storey pair is designed in Dutch style with the centre recessed. The building as a whole is rough-cast with brick quoins on ragstone plinths, steeply pitched roofs and rough-cast chimneystacks. Notable features include the leaded light casements.

Domestic Revival style Bayham Road

Leonard Williams designed his second pair in Domestic Revival style. Again rough-cast, including the six chimneystacks, but with timber framing to the first floor and end gables which also have projecting barge-boards. There are oriel windows on each gable and multi-light casements on the ground floor.

French Chateau style Bayham Road

The final pair of semi-detached properties were designed by Leonard Williams in an eye-catching French Chateau style with mansard tiled roofs and recessed centres. Notable features include the projecting end gables which have a large oculus.

BOWERWOOD HOUSE, ST BOTOLPH'S ROAD

Charles J Cable was a notable local architect whose work can be found on the Wildernesse estate, including the locally listed Red Gables (1926) and Silverley (1928), both in Woodland Rise. Cable's work can also be found elsewhere in Sevenoaks such as the locally listed property built for historian Hugh Wyatt Standen in Granville Road. In the 1920s, Charles Cable was commissioned by Dr James Harrison to design a purpose-built family home, surgery and museum. The locally listed Bowerwood House in St Botolph's Road was the result. It became the Harrison family home and surgical practice. It was also home to the 'Harrison Zoological Museum', now the registered scientific 'Harrison Institute', which Dr James Harrison himself founded and opened in 1930. Together with his two sons, Drs. Jeffery and David Harrison, Dr James Harrison carried out highly regarded nature conservation work. Dr Jeffery Harrison's subsequent work in establishing the Sevenoaks Wildlife Reserve is a particular example of pioneering nature conservation work.

Built in Arts & Crafts style, Bowerwood House is a two-storey detached timber-framed house under a half-hipped tiled roof. On the left, there is a projecting timber-framed gabled wing, jettied at first floor on carved brackets above a five-light canted bay window with a five-light window at the first floor. On the right, there are four-light windows at ground and first floor with a projecting entrance under a swept down roof.

Safeguarding Our Heritage

John Stambollouian & Keith Wade

It is the responsibility of the present generation to preserve our heritage for those to come: it is literally their inheritance, providing a sense of identity and continuity in our fast-changing world. However it is not just about protecting the past. Identifying, recording, maintaining and saving our historical and cultural fabric is of course vitally important. But so is encouraging excellence and innovation in the design of new developments that are necessary and appropriate for their setting.

Sevenoaks Capriccio by Peter Alchin

All communities must move with the times. There is a fine balance between saving the old and making way for the new. Difficult decisions have to be made. To a large extent we place our trust in the planning authorities to guard our heritage, to guide developers, architects, builders, and property owners, and impartially to assess their proposals and applications. Other safeguards are in place – but sometimes through neglect, lack of understanding, obsolescence, inappropriate development, accident or natural forces, important heritage assets are damaged or lost.

Heritage buildings, open spaces and other important items of the public realm are given protection from destruction or unsympathetic alteration in a number of ways and by various bodies:

LISTED BUILDINGS

Statutory listed buildings are buildings and structures that have been recognised as being of national importance for their special architectural, historic or social interest. The list is maintained by Historic England. Alterations or extensions require listed building consent in addition to planning permission. There are some 190 listed buildings and structures in Sevenoaks including 35 original gas lamp standards. Knole House and the surrounding garden wall are Grade I Listed; twelve are Grade II* Listed.

LOCAL LISTING

Buildings and other artefacts such as walls, post boxes and lamp posts which are of importance but not sufficiently distinguished to be worthy of national listing can be placed on a Local List. Although this conveys no additional statutory protection, where such a List exists, it is taken into account by the local authority in making planning decisions. The Local List for Sevenoaks has been developed in a collaboration between The Sevenoaks Society and Sevenoaks District Council.

A landmark project for the Society, it is the first joint venture of its kind in Kent. It was given particular impetus by the demolition of the popular Farmers pub, where permission for development was granted on appeal after it had been refused by the District Council. The planning inspector said that had the building been locally listed, this would have been a significant factor in making his decision. Despite various efforts to ensure appropriate and speedy development, the key site opposite the station remains derelict.

The locally listed Stone House in Victoria Road is a rare surviving example of an agricultural dwelling in the heart of Sevenoaks. It was probably built in the 17th century and later became incorporated into Covell's Farm.

NATIONAL HERITAGE LIST FOR ENGLAND

In addition to nationally listed buildings, this database maintained by Historic England also holds records of and provides protection for Registered Parks and Gardens (including Knole Park, Judd's Piece and the Upper High Street Gardens) and Scheduled Ancient Monuments (such as the Neolithic barrow in Millpond Wood).

CONSERVATION AREAS

Conservation areas are sites of special architectural or historic interest. Like listed buildings, they are an example of a Designated Heritage Asset, and form part of Sevenoaks' Historic Environment that the District Council seeks to conserve and enhance as a key element of its Local Plan. There are eight in Sevenoaks Town, including the whole of the High Street, which contains over one hundred listed buildings.

VOLUNTARY BODIES

As well as government institutions and large national organisations such as Historic England, National Trust, CPRE and English Heritage, an important role is played by local voluntary bodies such as conservation councils, heritage trusts and civic societies. The Sevenoaks Society's goal is "the conservation and improvement of the town", achieved through its monitoring of schemes, work with the local authorities, public statements and campaigns, and major projects such as the Local List.

OUR HERITAGE IS PRECIOUS

The Grade II White House (left) stood opposite the Red House in the High Street, with its Georgian front added to the original building in 1810. The photograph was taken in 1971, shortly before its demolition. Despite an Appeal, it was condemned by a planning inspector as unsafe and unsaveable, riddled with death watch beetle and dry rot.

This building replaced it.

THE RANGE OF HERITAGE ASSETS

Many of the heritage assets featured in the book are nationally or locally listed for their historical or cultural importance, architectural merit or amenity value. The further examples below illustrate the range of buildings on the Sevenoaks Local List.

Former Gasworks Site & Sanitary Laundry

Now a group of commercial units, these buildings date to the mid-19th century. Arranged around an open yard at the corner of Holly Bush Lane and Hartslands Road, they are surrounded by a ragstone wall which was the boundary of the original Sevenoaks gasworks established in 1838. They later became a laundry – a major source of employment in this working-class area.

Park Grange, High Street

The imposing and elegant ragstone mansion Park Grange was built in 1869 for the eminent railway engineer Sir George Berkley, on the site of Park Farm which he had bought with its nine acres of land. The house and substantial estate was bequeathed to Sevenoaks School by the Johnson Trustees in 1948.

This detached two-storey home of distinctive contemporary design demonstrates that buildings do not have to be old or historic to qualify as being worthy of recognition and protection.

Holly Bush Lane

Marking Our Heritage

Various plaques in Sevenoaks denote the architectural or historic value of a building, or commemorate notable figures or events associated with it. Several buildings in the historic Upper High Street have plaques issued by The Sevenoaks Society over the years. Some, with the emblematic Kent white horse, show that the building is listed. Others, on the Reeves House, the Red House railings, the Chantry and the almshouses, contain a brief description.

HG Wells is remembered by the HG Wells Society's blue plaque on no.23 Eardley Road where he wrote much of "The Time Machine". (Speaking of himself and other lodgers there, he warned: *"People with lodgings to let in Sevenoaks ought to know the sort of people who might take them."*).

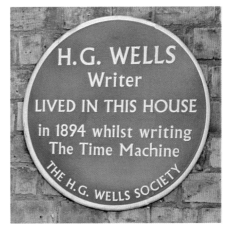

Sevenoaks also has a town heritage trail with embossed brass plaques set in the pavement as part of the Millennium Walk. The one to the left is outside 'The Reeve's House' at nos. 63 – 65 High Street

Encouraging and recognising good design

"Good design" is to some extent subjective, but in general it has the following characteristics: it is aesthetically pleasing, gives a "sense of place", serves its purpose, promotes sustainability, is meticulous in its attention to detail, and, importantly, is appropriate for its setting.

Sevenoaks District Council's Local Plan for 2015 – 2035 rightly places great emphasis on ensuring "high quality" design in development proposals – whatever their size, shape or form. The Design Principles within the Plan are criteria which all new developments must meet, and detailed guidance shows how this should be done.

A Sevenoaks Society's biennial award scheme seeks to encourage and recognise buildings and projects which best demonstrate excellence in design and construction quality, and make a positive impact on the public realm. The award was established in 2013 in memory of the late Frank Marshall who made an immense contribution to the work of the Society, the promotion of high quality design, and the conservation of the town's heritage.

The first award in 2013 was given to the extension of The Vine restaurant: a successful contemporary addition to a former mid-Victorian pub at a sensitive location close to the historic Vine cricket ground and within an important conservation area. The 2015 award was to Tricon House in Old Coffee House Yard, London Road. It was originally a tired-looking two-storey 1960s building of brick and tile. The property was refurbished, reclad in zinc and an additional storey added. It has been transformed in a way which is functional and contemporary but adds interest. The 2017 Award was given for the restoration of the medieval barn at Knole House and the alterations to the Brewhouse courtyard.

We all have a role to play in helping to conserve and improve our town, and to recognise and strive for high quality design. We hope this book has not only opened your eyes to the many treasures in Sevenoaks, but has increased your awareness of the vital need to cherish them – and so keep them safe, sound and secure for posterity.

BIBLIOGRAPHY

Aaron, Henry. Street furniture. Shire Publications, 1987

Anckorn, Gordon. A Sevenoaks camera. Ashgrove Press. 1979

Anckorn, Gordon. Sevenoaks memories. Ashgrove Press, 1984

Barty-King, Hugh. The New Beacon 1900-2000. New Beacon School, 2000

Bell, Christopher. The Catholic church of St Thomas of Canterbury. The author, 1996

Bolton, Mike. The almshouses and Sevenoaks School: A brief history. (n.d.)

Box E.G. Sevenoaks and adjoining parishes. Typescript. 1927

Building News. ' Thomas G Jackson'. Vol 71. 13 November, 1896

Burgess, Phillip. Then and now: Sevenoaks. Tempus , 2001

Cameron, Julia. St Nicholas: The church that went under. Paternoster, 1999

Carnell, George F. 'Old Sevenoaks'. Archaeologia Cantiana vol 23. 1898

Cufley, David. Brickmakers Index map. 2000

Davies, Philip. Troughs and drinking fountains. Chatto and Windus, 1989

Devereux, Charles. Railways to Sevenoaks. Oakwood Press, 1977

Donald, Archie. The posts of Sevenoaks. Woodvale, 1992.

Drive News Centenary issue. March 2004

Dunlop, John. The pleasant town of Sevenoaks. Holmesdale Press, 1964.

Edwards, Jane. Her recollections of old Sevenoaks. Sevenoaks Society, 1985

Evernden, Heather. 175 Years of Walthamstow Hall. The School, 2014

Fielding, C.H. The records of Rochester Diocese. West Kent Printing Works, 1910

Fox, Jean. History of Sevenoaks up to 1650. Magpie Technologies, 2002

Harper, Russell. Sevenoaks and around through time. Amberley Press, 2013

Hasted, Edward. History and topographical survey of Kent, Vol III. Bristow, 1797

Hetherington, Keith. 'Some prominent Kent brewers'. Bygone Kent. 1986. p.529-30

Hewlings, Richard. 'The School and almshouses at Sevenoaks'.

The Georgian Group Journal. Vol X1, 2001

Historic England. National Heritage List for England database

Hollybush Residents Association. Hollybush on the map. HRA, 1999

Horn, Pamela. Amusing the Victorians. Amberley Press,1999

Howell, Keith. Victorian and Edwardian Kent. Frith, 2002

Ingleton,Roy. Policing Kent 1800-2000. Phillimore,2002.

Jackson, Nicholas. Recollections of Sir Thomas Graham Jackson. Unicorn Press, 2003

Judd, Walter. Record of Wesleyan Methodism in the Sevenoaks Circuit.
Rush and Warwick, 1932

Kearns, Ann & Harper, Patrick. Ann Kearns' Sevenoaks. Foxprint Publications,1992

Kent compendium of historic parks and gardens. 2011-2013. KCC.

Killingray, David. 'A London city church estate in Kent: St Botolph's, Sevenoaks,
1646-2002'. Archaeologia Cantiana, Vol. 124, 2004

Killingray , David and **Purves**, Elizabeth. Sevenoaks; an historical dictionary.
Phillimore, 2012.

Killingray, David. Sevenoaks people and faith. Phillimore, 2004

Killingray, David. St Nicholas parish church: a brief history. The Church, 1990

Knocker, Herbert W. 'Sevenoaks. The manor, church and market'.
Archaeologia Cantiana Vol. 38, 1926

Knocker and Foskett. Records held by Knocker and Foskett.

Lansberry, H.C.F. Sevenoaks wills and inventories in reign of Charles II. K.A.S, 1988

Methodist Recorder. 7 April 1904

Metropolitan Drinking Fountain and Cattle Trough Association web site

Newman, John. Kent, West and the Weald. Yale U.P., 2012

Nunnerley, David. A history of Montreal Park. The author, 2000.

Obituary**.** James **German**. Sevenoaks Chronicle. 1 November 1901

Obituary. Lilian Gilchrist **Thompson**. Sevenoaks Chronicle. 6 June 1947

Obituary. Lilian Gilchrist **Thompson**. The Times.9 June 1947

Obituary. Edward **Kraftmeier**. Sevenoaks Chronicle. January 1917

Obituary. Emily **Jackson**. The Times. 22 December 1916

Obituary. Thomas G **Jackson**. Sevenoaks Chronicle. 11 November,1924

Obituary. Francis **Swanzy**. Sevenoaks Chronicle. 14 May 1920

Obituary. William J **Thompson**. Sevenoaks Chronicle. 22 April 1904

Ogley, Bob and Perkins, Roger. Sevenoaks Chronicle of the century. Froglets, 1999

Oxford Dictionary of National Biography. Oxford University Press, 2004

Parish, R.B. 'Lock-ups of Kent'. Bygone Kent.Vol 17. No 4.

Parkin, Monty. The story of Sevenoaks Market. Kemsing Heritage Centre, 2009

Parliamentary Select Committee. Minutes of Evidence on the state of children
employed manufacturies. 1816

Pike, Elsie. The story of Walthamstow Hall. Longmore Press, 1973

Rayner, Christopher. Sevenoaks past. Phillimore, 1997

Raynor, Brian. John Frith, scholar and martyr. Hawthorns Publications, 2000

Richards, Frank. Old Sevenoaks. Salmon, 1901

Robinson, Martin. Old letter boxes. Shire Publications, 1987

Rooker, John. Parish church of St Nicholas. Salmon, 1910

Sackville-West, Robert. Inheritance: the story of Knole. Bloomsbury, 2010

Sackville-West, Robert. Knole. National Trust, 2006

Sackville-West, Vita. Knole. National Trust, 1950

Salmon's Guide to Sevenoaks and the neighbourhood, Salmon, 1901 onwards

Salmon's Directory, Sevenoaks. Salmon, 1903 onwards

Scragg, Brian. Sevenoaks School, a history. Ashgrove Press, 1993

The Sevenoaks Chronicle. 1881 onwards

Sevenoaks District Council. Conservation Area Appraisal. Sevenoaks High Street. SDC, 2008

Sevenoaks District Council. Conservation Area Appraisal. Brittains Farm. SDC, 2011

Sevenoaks Gas Company. Early history of the gas works.

Papers compiled from Sevenoaks Gas Company records at C.K.S. (n.d.)

Sevenoaks Society. Sir John Dunlop's History Notes. The Sevenoaks Society, 1994

Sevenoaks Society. The Local List. The Sevenoaks Society, 2018

Sevenoaks Society. Town centre surveys. The Sevenoaks Society, 1980-97

Sevenoaks Society. 100 Years growth in Sevenoaks. The Sevenoaks Society, 1994

Sevenoaks Town Council. Kraftmeier Mauseleum Leaflet. (n.d)

Smart, K.J. Cricket on the Vine. Sevenoaks Vine Cricket Club, 1983

Standen, H.W. Kippington in Kent. The author, 1958

Stoyel, Anthony. Report on the history of 101 High Street Sevenoaks. Sevenoaks District Architectural History Group, 1984

Stoyel, Anthony. 'The Clockhouse'. Sevenoaks Society Newsletter. Autumn 1998.

Terry, Ron. Cyfartha Castle and Bradbourne Hall. Typescript, 2005

Terry, Ron. Old corners of Sevenoaks. Caxton & Holmesdale Press, 2000

Thompson, Ed . Sevenoaks recollections. Circa Publishing. 1994

Thompson, Ed and Clucas, Philip. Sevenoaks - the past in pictures. Hopgarden Press, 2010

Thompson, Ed and Clucas, Philip . St John's - the past in pictures. Hopgarden Press, 2013

Vigar, John. The Drinking Fountain Association in Kent. Bygone Kent. Vol 5,1984, p. 596-599

Ward, Gordon. Sevenoaks essays. Ashgrove Press, 1980

ELIZABETH PURVES

Elizabeth has lived in Sevenoaks for 30 years and was the Local Studies and Reference Librarian at Sevenoaks Library. She has also represented her area as a District Councillor for the past 12 years. With colleagues, she has written three books, *Hollybush on the Map*, *Sevenoaks: An Historical Dictionary* and *Sevenoaks Forgotten Past: Lodges and Coach Houses*. A member of the Selection Panel for the recently produced Sevenoaks Local List, she is committed to promoting and preserving our local heritage, and hopes this book will encourage people to take a greater interest in our town's history.

GERALDINE TUCKER

A History graduate, Geraldine began her career in the Foreign & Commonwealth Office and later transferred to the Ministry of Defence. Her final posting was in the Cabinet Office, working on international affairs. Geraldine has lived in Sevenoaks for almost 30 years and is on the Sevenoaks Society's Executive Committee. She headed the research team for the Sevenoaks Local List. In 2017, she co-authored the local history book '*Sevenoaks Forgotten Past: Lodges & Coach Houses*'. Geraldine is the leader of the Society's 2019 'Sevenoaks Heritage Exhibition'.

KEITH WADE

Keith has been an Officer of The Sevenoaks Society for several years and in 2014/5 was responsible for the Society's exhibitions on The Remarkable Trees of Sevenoaks. After graduating with a degree in Classics, and then qualifying as an accountant, Keith spent most of his career in education, training and writing. Following his move to Sevenoaks in 1984, he established an international training consultancy specialising in business control and audit, operating in Africa, the Caribbean, Europe, and the Middle and Far East.